Training
the High School
Orchestra

CARSON ROTHROCK

PARKER PUBLISHING COMPANY, INC.
West Nyack, N.Y.

© 1971 BY

PARKER PUBLISHING COMPANY, INC.

WEST NYACK, N.Y.

LIBRARY OF CONGRESS
CATALOG CARD NUMBER: 71-148489

PRINTED IN THE UNITED STATES OF AMERICA
ISBN 0-13-926816-2
B&P

WHAT THIS BOOK OFFERS

The teacher of a junior high or high school orchestra is an extremely busy person, exerting every effort to have his orchestra play music well. This book contains many ideas and procedures for use with the school orchestra that will help achieve this goal.

Tested ideas are offered in areas from dealing with students to using visual aids. Along with these are convenient check lists for routine procedures that will make the daily work easier and teaching more efficient.

Along with teaching procedures that are especially adapted for use with an orchestra, there are chapters on procedure dealing with full orchestra rehearsal, lessons in general, instruction of wind instrument players, string lessons, and the important consideration of percussion teaching.

Interesting ways of using the tape recorder as a teaching tool and many visual aids that help in teaching various aspects of the subject are described. A list of helpful reference books that should be in every music department library is included. Other chapters deal with selecting music, selecting equipment, and arranging the details for presenting performances.

The advantage of this book is that I am a working orchestra director in a typical school system. Years of experience have provided me with many solutions to the problems encountered in the quest for a better-sounding orchestra. The ideas I present have been tested and proven with average students who practice an average amount, most of them unaided by private lessons. Philosophical discussions are avoided because I assume that the reader has already been convinced of the value of the orchestral experience.

—Carson Rothrock

I wish to express my gratitude to my friend and colleague, Mr. Lloyd Snyder, director of the Ewing High School Orchestra, for reviewing the entire manuscript. I also wish to thank Professor Arthur Frank of Temple University, who was kind enough to check Chapter 10 for technical accuracy.

CONTENTS

Chapter 7: *Equipping the Orchestra* • 95

Obtaining equipment; music; chairs; music stands; instruments; maintenance and replacement; selection of instruments; accessories; teaching aids; office equipment; rehearsal room equipment; practice room equipment; storage facilities; auditorium equipment.

Chapter 8: *Improving the String Section* • 109

Balancing the section; tuning the instrument; reviewing fundamental left hand technique; teaching the fingerboard; the changing clef for viola and cello; vibrato; orchestral bowing.

Chapter 9: *Preparing Orchestral Wind Players* • 133

The soloistic nature of orchestral wind playing; instrumental proficiency: phrasing, rhythm, intonation, technique, tone quality; vibrato; reserve wind players; maintenance and repair.

Chapter 10: *The Percussion Section* • 149

The percussion player; percussion equipment; percussion PRITT skills; percussion lesson procedure; maintenance.

Chapter 11: *The Problem of Ensemble* • 165

Building ensemble; rhythm; tempo; balance; phrasing; bowing; intonation; tone color.

Chapter 12: *Conductor's Problems* • 177

The conductor's personality; conducting motions; helping uncertain players; learning the score; professional improvement.

Chapter 13: *Using Teaching Aids* • 189

Effective use of teaching aids; choosing a teaching aid: words, demonstrations, chalkboard, charts, mock-ups, recordings, videotape, tuners, rhythm trainers, motion pictures; the orchestra as a teaching aid.

Chapter 14: *Public Performances* • 205

Scheduling performances; the concert program; stage fright; soloists; youth concerts; the orchestra tour; the pit orchestra; festival performances; publicity.

***Index* • 225**

1 ORCHESTRA PERSONNEL

The human factor involved in teaching orchestra is a prime consideration for improving the music. The director must use all the methods at his command for bringing out the results he wants from the students he has selected as orchestra members. The criticism he offers, the encouragement he gives, and the obedience he demands are all important psychological aids toward bettering the music.

The student-teacher relationship

As a student comes to your orchestra for the first time, it is a special event for both of you. If things turn out well, he will spend several years learning music under your guidance. He will know you better than any other teacher in the school. You will know him better than his guidance counselor. During the rest of his life, this student will remember his days under your baton each time he hears an orchestra play.

This special relationship of orchestra member to orchestra director is what guides you in your teaching techniques, your choice of words in correcting the student, and in your decisions about what experiences he should undergo. It is a seesaw relationship with the student on one end, you on the other, and musical matters in the middle. To handle it properly, you need to know the musical background and aptitude of each student, his general attitude toward playing and toward orchestra. Knowing this will help you to know when to be severe, when to coax, and when to demand.

Evaluating students' readiness for orchestra

Previous orchestral experience is the most valuable asset a student can bring to you. It is a basic foundation from which you can build. Band experience is good preparation, but it will take time for him to become accustomed to the differences. A background of private lessons indicates the player is serious about his instrument and probably well-grounded in the fundamentals. Without one or more of these prior experiences, the student will flounder for a time in orchestra. If there are only a few of these inexperienced players, they can be put in the orchestra to "sink or swim," since nothing nurtures orchestral playing faster than the experience of sitting in with a group of seasoned players. Care must be taken to seat the novices beside strong players who will not be led astray by errors the new players make. If there are many incoming students in the inexperienced category, a preparatory orchestra is needed. Here they can learn orchestral procedure step by step without slowing down an advanced group.

In addition to knowing the groups and teachers with whom a prospective student has played and studied, you will want to know the results of any musical aptitude tests he has taken. These results will point up areas in which the student has difficulty, and they will give you an idea what to expect from him musically. Tests of this kind are definitely desirable in advising a student contemplating a musical career. For all the above reasons, it is worth the time to administer such a test if it has not been done previously.

The quickest way you can evaluate the skill a student has derived from his previous musical activities is to hear him play privately. However, such an audition is frightening to anybody, and a young person inexperienced in such things will shy away from it, even to the extent that many would choose not to play in the orchestra rather than undergo an entrance audition. Auditions are a part of a musician's life, and it is good education for a student to experience many of them, but they are best delayed until the student feels reasonably secure in the orchestra and at ease with the teacher. Otherwise, the member-director relationship may fracture before it begins.

The attitude of a student toward playing his instrument and toward orchestra in general can be estimated if you know the extent of his musical involvement in and out of school. His guidance counselors, parents, and former music teachers could provide much helpful information, but an interview with the student himself is more expedient than searching out the other people, and it serves as a get-acquainted session.

The initial interview

You will want your first interview to allay any fears the student may have about joining the orchestra. Emphasize the positive aspects, such as the rewarding experiences he has had before in music. Let him know that many who had been apprehensive went on to become valuable orchestra members. Name names and show pictures; he may know some of the people involved, and this makes what you have to tell him more meaningful. Promise that you'll understand if he has problems with the music and that you'll help him. Be careful; if you promise him an easy time of it, he may take you at your word and do no work at all to try to increase his musical ability; if you stress the need for much outside practice, he will worry about the demand on his after-school time. Really, the amount he will have to practice depends upon: (1) the amount and quality of his prior musical experiences, (2) how perceptive he is musically, and (3) how skilled he is technically on his instrument.

The student who expresses no fears about joining your orchestra needs a careful interview also. It may be that he doesn't care about orchestra, in which case he must be won over to a more enthusiastic attitude as the year progresses. Another student may be extremely confident and enthusiastic, the kind we like to get, but he needs an interview if only so you can explain to him that not everyone feels as he does. Such a student mustn't expect musical miracles to be accomplished, but he must be convinced that the better he plays, the better the rest of the orchestra will play. The truth of this matter is that some players learn mostly by ear. These weaker readers learn after hearing the others play it through a few times. A musically confident orchestra member is in a position of responsibility where he must always play his best.

The initial interview starts the student-teacher relationship on a personal basis. From it you can gain first-hand knowledge of the problems, fears, and expectations of a student. The student

learns in the interview what will be expected of him. The more
the director knows about each member, the better he can work
with his orchestra. Such knowledge can be gained from available
written records and from interviews with the student and the people who know him.

Selecting orchestra members

Suppose twice your preferred number of clarinetists want to
join the orchestra. Should the more experienced players be selected, the older players, the younger players, the better scholars,
the ones who fare better in a ten-minute audition, the ones who
own better instruments, or should the balance of the orchestra be
sacrificed by accepting all?

Education is supposed to serve the students, and a guidance
counselor might ask you to accept all, but it is in the best interest
of each student to sit in a balanced orchestra. Everybody who
hears the orchestra perform deserves to hear a proper proportion
of each instrument.

Which of the players should make up this hypothetical clarinet
section? The inexperienced player and the player of whose cooperation you are not sure are likely candidates for elimination.
Students who know two instruments can play their minor instrument and in so doing perhaps fill a need. A player may be willing
to change instruments in order to play in the orchestra. This is a
prime source of players for the color instruments which are only
found in high school. Given a few months, a hard-working clarinet player can become an acceptable double-reed player. Given
a year, he can switch to an instrument of a different family. Some
clarinetists would enjoy being in the string section of an orchestra.

Hopefully, after some change instruments you will be left
with the proper number. If not, such matters as the age of the
player may have a bearing. The older student deserves to play in
the orchestra before he graduates, all other things being equal;
however, a younger player with the advantage of private lessons
is a logical first choice.

A private entrance audition is often inconclusive, not only because of the player's fright mentioned earlier, but because it is
impossible in this setting to assess a player's ability to adapt his
playing to the rest of the orchestra. If some players must be eliminated by audition, schedule them all for orchestra temporarily.

After they feel relatively at ease in the orchestra, have them take turns playing with the orchestra passages that feature their instrument. After this "under-fire" audition, there will be little doubt in anyone's mind about who should play the part.

In short, procedures for dealing with an oversupply of players for any section are: (1) eliminate inexperienced players and ones whose interest in orchestra is doubtful, (2) have some play their minor instrument, (3) have some change instruments, (4) choose those with private lessons, (5) choose the older student, all else being equal, and (6) use "under-fire" auditions.

The size of the orchestra influences decisions about how many can be accepted in each section. You may be shocked some year to come up with the full symphonic instrumentation you always dreamed of, only to find that all the players can't possibly squeeze onto your stage. That's a remote possibility and a problem we all would like to face, but some crowding problems do occur under normal circumstances which require personnel adjustment. A pianist may not be selected because of a lack of room for the instrument on the stage with the orchestra. Pianists are needed in the instrumental music program, however, and they should be able to earn credit for their musical work the same as any other instrumentalist. They can accompany solos, play chamber music, and all of them would enjoy playing the harpsichord with the string orchestra. Of course, if a pianist becomes earnest about playing in the full orchestra, he will be able to learn a second instrument fast enough to be of great use. Then too, he'll be on hand to play xylophone, celesta, or bell parts if necessary.

A large orchestra with full instrumentation is a fine group to work with when everyone is busy. Due to differences in orchestration, there are many compositions that have no parts for certain players. The players of these parts will not be able to sustain an interest in a work in which they're not at all involved. Tacit players should be permitted to study schoolwork; they're earning their credit in the same way the symphony tubaist earns his salary. This subject has to do with selecting members, because a person who is often tacit could become a discipline problem. The orchestra, having a difficult task and a large number of members, cannot withstand the strain of a misbehaving student. Any benefit he derives from the orchestra is really stolen bit by bit from the richer experience the other players would have if he were not there. It must be made clear to students upon selection that they will not be permitted to interfere with the rehearsal in any way. Selecting many auxiliary players who will be tacit during a majority of compositions is likely to cause serious discipline problems. If a player can't be used most of the time, it is better not to select him.

Recruiting players

Finding enough players for the orchestra is a more common problem than finding ways to utilize surplus players. The initial interview, discussed earlier, many times turns into a selling effort. Fear of a new situation leads a student to have misgivings about selecting a course that is not career-connected or otherwise mandatory. Also there may be other reasons: a feeling of inadequacy on the instrument, a wish to concentrate on studies, a feeling of guilt about spending time and effort on an unrequired course, a dissatisfaction with prior experiences in orchestra, a special ambition in other areas, pressure toward other areas from parents or friends, or a desire to go along with the crowd and schedule what they are taking.

In the initial interview you can do the things suggested before: emphasize the positive aspects of his former and prospective orchestra membership; let him know case histories of people with his problems; promise help and understanding. And you can go further by pointing out what he already knows about the technique of his instrument, the reading of music, following a conductor, etc. Let him know what additional things he will learn by continuing: different music, a higher level of performance, and a better understanding of music. The fringe benefits are important to him, also. The pleasure of playing music, the break that it offers from book study, and trips the orchestra takes are incentives for the student to continue. Show him pictures and let him hear tapes of your orchestra so that he can compare the experiences he's had with the richer ones you're offering.

The student may point out problems that make it difficult for him to elect orchestra. Scheduling that forces a student to have to choose between orchestra and any other one subject should be changed if at all possible.

Musical organizations often conflict in scheduling. The students have to choose between instrumental and vocal training. Most want to continue with both and some provision for this could be made by scheduling groups during study periods or off school time whereby the students could pursue their second choice of musical activity.

Another problem that students have is pressure from home and from guidance counselors. A conference with parents is desirable in such a case so that you can convince them of the value of the orchestra program. They must see the value of it for their child's well-being and liberal education.

The orchestra director must work hand-in-glove with the guidance department to make sure the students are being advised correctly and well regarding orchestra in their schedule. In being overly zealous about planning courses to prepare a student for his future career, a guidance counselor may neglect to provide for the general education and present needs of the student. Multiple possibilities of scheduling may be overlooked by a counselor when he sees that an easy answer to a problem is to eliminate orchestra from a student's schedule. He will try harder if he knows you will request a detailed explanation when any such thing occurs. Collect statements from students and recent graduates about what the orchestra meant to them. Let the guidance department hear what these people had to say. Keep counselors informed of how orchestra is helping those presently enrolled, and express your appreciation for the part guidance plays in making it possible to schedule the students into orchestra. Guidance personnel will be on your side if you show that you have each student's welfare in mind.

Despite all your efforts, some students will not elect orchestra. They are losing a valuable emotional and educational experience. Knowing this, you are tempted to coax them into joining, but this is a little like asking them to eat a meal they don't want. Don't worry about prospective players who don't sign up; it's their loss more than yours, and you don't want a person in the orchestra who doesn't want to be there. Later they may change their minds and come to you, especially if orchestra members tell them that players of their instrument are needed. However, if you succeed in coaxing someone to join orchestra, that person will feel that he is doing you a favor by being there.

Rehearsal atmosphere

Working with his knowledge of each student, the director can proceed to form an atmosphere in the rehearsal that is conducive to learning musical literature. The teacher and students work together seriously, building a musical performance. The only fun connected to it is the thrill of playing music. Some days the difficulties can make the rehearsal a miserable experience, but this only heightens the feeling of accomplishment when the difficulties are surmounted.

The serious working atmosphere can be ruined by one recalcitrant player. If that player really doesn't want to be there, if he doesn't share the desire for producing a good performance, you are better off without him. No matter what his musical skills may be, the uncooperative student must be dropped before the attitude spreads.

The morale of the orchestra depends greatly on the atmosphere of the rehearsal. Discipline must be maintained during the actual rehearsal so that the work can be accomplished and the music learned, but in the moments between numbers the players can relax physically and mentally. They will play better after a short rest. When explanation becomes necessary, they can relax physically while listening. Playing constantly tires players, and it leads to poor posture, poor playing, and a careless approach to the notes. However, a long explanation bores the players, and they tend to miss the important points. For this reason, too much playing is better than too much explanation. The morale of the orchestra will not be hurt by a rehearsal in which the members feel that they are the main participants.

There are many times when drilling a section on a passage can't be avoided. This is a dead spot in the rehearsal for the rest of the orchestra. Though the others realize the need, they may fail to cooperate. They may talk, play their instrument, shuffle feet, etc. There are things they can learn during this time, and these things should be pointed out to them. First of all, the same passage may happen in their part at another time, so they should be listening. Second, they can learn much about musical performance by watching and listening to the progress of the drill. Third, if they can't remain interested in the drill, they can at least be polite and not interfere. Unless the drill is prolonged, most students will be aware of the improvement of the passage and learn to appreciate the contributions of the orchestra members outside their own section.

Praise vs. condemnation

During drilling sessions many players will develop feelings of ineptitude and insecurity. Any time such feelings are evident, the conductor must be encouraging. To be severe at such a time would only make the student feel hopelessly inadequate. We must develop the confidence of insecure players so that they will be able to keep up with the rest of the orchestra. This is not to say that we should accept poor playing; there is a definite need for condemnation. If a passage is not played correctly, the students must know for certain that it is unacceptable. The time for condemnation of a passage is before drilling on it; for instance, "Cellos, that passage will not do; let's work on it a while." Then, after drilling it a number of times: "That's better, and I think you understand what's wrong with the passage now. With more drill and some individual work on it, it ought to be all right." Through this approach, the insecure player learns: (1) the passage is important, (2) he can't play it as it should be, (3) he made some improvement, so practice does help, and (4) he'll be given another chance to rehearse it with the group. The following week some encouragement for further work could be given along with a remark about the improvement that the work so far had made.

An individual player gets disgusted with himself for ruining a passage. The conductor must acknowledge the fact that it happened. You can do this by a raised eyebrow, a shake of the head, or a short lecture; but to disregard it will only lead the student to conclude that it isn't important. What's worse, he might get the feeling that you aren't listening closely. This attitude on the part of a student leads to careless playing. If he feels you will let him get by with a sloppy rendition of his part, he won't go through the work of perfecting it.

So there is a definite need for condemnation. Of course it is the playing that is being condemned, not the player. "You'll never make a musician," and other such remarks start personality conflicts that add unnecessary tension to the rehearsal atmosphere. Even if the purpose of such a statement is to challenge the stu-

dent to prove you wrong, its value is questionable considering the
harm it may do.

All orchestra personnel, secure and insecure, need praise to
keep them eager. This praise is best limited to details most of the
time, e.g., "The bowing is very neat in the passage we just played;
good work." If you just say, "Good," what is the flutist to think who
missed the cue and didn't play? What will the hornist think who
knows he played a few wrong notes? Indiscriminate praise is almost without value. Sometimes the habit of linking praise with
condemnation can lessen the effect of the encouraging statement;
for instance, "Good dynamics, but the notes are too short." Nothing is wrong with this statement unless the form becomes such a
pattern that the orchestra members cringe every time they are
complimented because they expect a remonstrance immediately
afterward. A slightly different wording can help. Instead of the
negative sounding "but," "and let's also" could be used. This is a
small point of semantics, hardly worth mentioning, except for the
fact that as we are working with emotional individuals, we must
use every means at our disposal to build a positive attitude toward
the task we are trying to accomplish.

Humor in the rehearsal relaxes, refreshes, and makes the hard
work more enjoyable. Some conductors try too hard in this area,
mimicking the playing of a particular section as a form of condemnation. To make fun of the playing of a section demoralizes
its members, and this type of humor is not really appreciated by
the rest of the orchestra. Enough fun can be had in natural situations, when everyone can join in the laughter.

Maintaining an objective attitude

As you learn to know a student during the year, you may let
your personal feelings toward him color your judgments about his
playing. The only way objectivity can be maintained is by keeping musical matters foremost in your mind as you listen to a student perform. Musically, it doesn't matter who is playing, or how
hard he is trying, or how much he has practiced. Musically, it
really doesn't matter that he has made an improvement since yesterday. As teachers we praise improvement, but as musicians we
are impatient with any performance that is not what we want it
to be. If this impatience shows from time to time, it will let the
students know the job is not done.

The student's emotions interfere with his judgment about his own performance. He has a difficult time being objective about his playing. One aid to let him hear his playing as others hear it is to record. By his remarks after the playback, you may suspect that he isn't hearing himself objectively as he plays. This is a common ailment—maybe because teachers push for technique, occupying the student's mind with the notes to come rather than the ones that have been played—but eventually the player must be able to evaluate his performance as it takes place.

Some players with good scholastic ability have trouble producing good musical results because their minds are centered on following instructions. They try too hard and produce exaggerated effects in an attempt to put a teacher's advice to work. The best approach to this type of student is a non-technical one: "Let the melodic line flow," or, "Relax the phrase as you approach the high note,"—anything to help him concentrate on the sound instead of the machine in his hands.

Encouraging instrumental progress

All students can benefit by an experimental approach to their instrument. Let them enjoy the discovery of how music works. A string player who figures out a passage in fourth position for himself will be much more impressed with it than he would be if he found the fingerings marked in his part. The compassionate teacher who edits music by inserting fingerings, eliminating sixteenth notes, transposing parts for wind players, cutting out difficult sections, etc., is building a performance but cheating the students of a part of their musical education. These procedures must be used to keep the material within the capabilities of the players in order to make a presentable performance, but first the students deserve a chance to stumble, investigate, and try to master the music in its original form.

When the students request more guidance in their experimentation, advise them to take private lessons from a qualified player. From such a person they can learn shortcuts to better performance. We as directors are being selfish if we push students into private lessons just because we want a better orchestra, but the advantages of them should be pointed out to each student. No one must feel that he is a second-class orchestra member because he doesn't take private lessons, especially since many players with only school lessons develop into better players than those who have had several years of private instruction. The point that students must know is that the attention of the best available teacher in a private situation is required in order to bring an individual's musical skills as far as possible.

Authority of the conductor

Personality characteristics sometimes interfere with the smooth operation of an orchestra. Certain people don't want to sit beside others, some get angry because they think they deserve to be advanced in seating, etc. The conductor can do much to curb these conflicts by taking steps to prevent their occurrence and by asserting his authority to resolve disputes.

One of the most troublesome attitudes is that of the "prima donna." Avoid confrontations with this type of individual in front of the group; differences of opinion should be discussed in private. If the person is talented, he will be pleased with the challenge of a solo; this will provide a chance for him to utilize his interpretive skills.

Seating considerations should be purely musical. Getting along with each other in the group situation is one thing the students ought to learn, but some disagreements must be resolved by the teacher. For example, suppose the playing position of one player interferes with that of another. It is up to the teacher to check on this and enforce a minimum standard from which no one may deviate. The appearance of the orchestra has an effect on the audience, and the position has an effect on the playing. Therefore, it is in the teacher's domain to resolve conflicts that arise in these matters.

Another thing that bothers players is a musical "helper" in the orchestra. The foot tapper and the shusher are assistants that the conductor must silence. Their hissing and tapping sounds come out above the sound of the orchestra and ruin the musical effect completely, whereas the sounds they mean to correct will be of lesser consequence. The root of the matter is that in trying to help, these people are usurping the conductor's authority. By demanding full control over the orchestra, the conductor is steering it on a course of musical improvement and also preventing some conflicts that might arise within the group.

2 SCHEDULING THE PERSONNEL

The primary need of the school orchestra player is instruction. There are five logical ways of providing it: (1) a part of each full orchestra rehearsal is set aside for instruction, (2) each family of instruments has a separate large group lesson, (3) similar instruments have instruction in small groups, (4) each student gets a short private lesson, (5) chamber music groups are scheduled for rehearsals, part of which can be used for instruction. You must work out the schedule, since only you know how best to group the students. Which of the above methods you use depends upon your personal preference and your local situation. The school schedule may be set up in such a way as to preclude the possibility of using any one of the five ways and a combination of them may be adopted. Some teachers are at their best teaching individuals, some teaching small groups, and some need the stimulation a large group provides. Before you place yourself in any one of these categories, investigate the possibilities of the five methods.

Five methods of grouping

1. Full rehearsals have the advantage of the better players, who produce the desired result for the others to copy. This speeds up instruction and makes it less tedious. One difficulty is finding material to play that is applicable for all instruments. The main

27

disadvantage is that the instruction cannot be made pertinent to every student. What is easy for some will be incomprehensible to others. Explanations to the latter will consume much rehearsal time. Technical advice to players of any one type of instrument must be held to a minimum for the same reason. An advantage to the orchestra lesson is that the application of technical principles to real music can readily be demonstrated. Otherwise, this method has little to recommend it, and the haphazard instruction that students are likely to derive from it is almost without value to their instrumental progress.

2.   Students grouped by families of instruments can work on common problems. True, tonguing on the flute is different from tonguing on the clarinet, but at least the use of the bow doesn't enter the picture during a woodwind lesson. The instruction can be more applicable in a family-grouped lesson, and a sectional rehearsal is possible. Disadvantages are those of a large group: individuals who have trouble get frustrated and those who don't get bored. Finding instructional material can be troublesome.

3.   Small groups playing the same type of instrument can get technical instruction without wasting anyone's time. Skilled players needn't be in a class with those less skilled. Materials are easy to find, and systematic progress is possible. Part of each period can be used to rehearse orchestra music. The students can study a solo for their instrument, and it can be analyzed in detail. Disadvantages are those of a small group: the orchestra music can't be rehearsed with continuity; the lesson often dwells on the weaknesses of one member of the group; absence of one player delays progress; and teaching intonation is a problem due to the lack of a musical texture to which the students can refer during playing to maintain the tonality. Chamber music for like instruments is limited, but it should be used because of the opportunity it provides to work on intonation.

4.   Working with a student privately is the best way to get to the root of his instrumental problems. All instruction can be made pertinent, and materials are easy to find. Solos can be used as training for musical interpretation and instrumental technique. All that's needed is an accompanist to make a full musical experience. The shortness of the lesson is the main disadvantage to private work in school.

5.   Chamber music ensembles are small groups of diversified

instruments. The advantages of the large group and the small group are present without most of the drawbacks that come with either. The musical discipline found in playing chamber music is better than any other because each student has complete responsibility for his part rhythmically and tonally. He soon finds that playing by ear will not work, and he learns to rely on his reading. Later he learns to use his ear in relating his part tonally to the sounds of the other instruments.

The quality of the training to be had in playing chamber music is the chief advantage of this type of grouping. The possibility of the immediate application of a technical principle to a musical setting is another advantage. Still another is the continuity with which the orchestra music can be played—many orchestral works can be played by a string quartet with no breaks due to a long rest in all parts. Ensemble grouping also enables the teacher to hear each student's performance clearly. It is easy to discern what mistake was made and by which player when the instruments are all different.

One disadvantage is the problem of discussing individual notes with players of transposing instruments. When you speak of concert A-flat, the horn player must know that it is E-flat for him, and the trumpet player must know it is B-flat in his part. This slows down a class somewhat, but it is good education and leads to more knowledgeable orchestra members. Another disadvantage is that the absence of one member makes playing chamber music impossible for that day, unless the teacher is able to sit in and play the missing part.

Scheduling groups for instruction

Which of the above methods of grouping students you adopt depends partially upon how well you can reconcile it with what your administration has already set up. If all students' schedules are full, you can arrange instruction on a rotating basis, whereby the student comes to you for a lesson from a different class each week. If students have study periods, you may want to arrange lessons during that time. The rotating schedule gives you complete freedom in grouping the students; assigning groups from study periods will work out as you would like only in a few cases. Grouping methods 2, 3, and 5, above, require the use of a rotating schedule.

If you schedule students from their study period, it is a good idea never to have that study period show on their schedule. Form the groups before the schedules are printed, so that "Instrumental Music" appears where you want it on their schedules. Otherwise, much of your lesson time may be spent in shepherding stray lambs from study halls.

Students can also be scheduled to come to you for purposes other than instruction instead of going to a study period. Practice time should be scheduled for players of the larger instruments. There's no use in having these people lug the instrument home if they can practice in school. Pianists can be scheduled to come to your room to provide accompaniment for a soloist or to join in playing chamber music. Chamber music groups from the orchestra may be formed of students available from a study hall, and these groups could rehearse without the need for the teacher's direct supervision.

Also available from study periods are office helpers. Students planning a business career can help you with your paperwork. It is good experience for them, a timesaver for you, and the improved organization of your office will be refreshing. Orchestra members are especially helpful because they require less explanation for jobs that have to do with music.

Even if you're working with a rotating schedule, add a provision for people to come from study periods in order to practice, to help in the office, to accompany solos, or to rehearse chamber music.

Scheduling rehearsals

Full orchestra rehearsal must be a permanent item in the schedule for best results. Rotating or off-school-time rehearsals lead to a high rate of absenteeism and drop-outs. A good schedule is one that discourages no one from participating because of the difficulty of attending. The best way is to have orchestra scheduled as a regular subject. The number of rehearsals per week depends upon the length of the rehearsal, the number of programs to be prepared, and the requirements for credit according to state standards. Needless to say, rehearsals beyond the minimum necessary for credit will increase the skill with which the music is played. Daily rehearsal is ideal, and it is not unrealistic, considering the difficulty of the task. Three rehearsals a week are satisfactory if the rehearsals are a full hour long. Any less than this tends to water down the education the pupils receive because little valuable musical literature can be undertaken without adequate rehearsal time.

A training orchestra for those with insufficient background to play in the regular orchestra can be put on the schedule. This B orchestra will have few performance obligations, so not as much rehearsal time is needed for it as for the A orchestra. If credit is given for the B orchestra, the number of meetings per week can be set at the mandated minimum. Students who are switching or beginning on instruments should be put in the B orchestra as soon as possible in their playing career—a sort of on-the-job training. Preferably, the B orchestra will be much smaller than the A, because the students in it need more careful supervision to prevent the formation of bad playing habits.

In addition to full orchestra and preparatory orchestra in the schedule, string orchestra is a valuable experience. Here the player learns to be independent from the winds and to project a true string tone. Sectional rehearsals of the strings improve the orchestra music greatly because the strings are the heart of it—as the string section goes, so goes the orchestra. Scheduling the winds elsewhere one or two days a week would not hurt the orchestra. This way the winds don't have to be bored while the strings drill on intonation and bowing. String orchestra literature can be played during these periods also. In this music the strings find the real expression of which their instruments are capable. Besides having a rich musical experience, the players learn bowings and fingerings that are useful in the full orchestra.

Sectional rehearsals

All sections of the orchestra sometimes require special attention that exceeds what is possible during the regular rehearsal. The other players can be given a study period during orchestra in order to accomplish this, or the sectional can be held before or after school. Of course, neither of these procedures need be used if the sectional lesson grouping is used. This consideration is not a major recommendation for that grouping, however; sectional rehearsals are needed weekly only by the strings. Auditions during sectional rehearsals are effective and quick. A player will prepare his parts carefully when auditions in front of a group are held frequently.

Free periods

One item that zealous teachers omit from their schedules is un-assigned time. True, the number of students in each lesson should be as small as possible, and teachers want to provide instruction for all who desire it; but it is in the interest of a better orchestra program to take time during the day to handle administrative details. The people who must be contacted for various services and decisions are seldom available after school. Planning rehearsals and lessons is better done during the school day also, leaving after-school time for special rehearsals or lessons.

Some time on the teacher's schedule can be freed by not duplicating a lesson for those students who obtain lessons privately outside of school. These students will appreciate not having their schedule altered, and the private teacher will respond favorably to the trust placed in his work.

Sample schedules

The preceding ideas are illustrated in the sample schedules of Tables 1–4. Not shown are after-school activities: chamber orchestra, soloist rehearsal, faculty meetings, sectional rehearsals, extra individual help, and the other myriad things that can or must be done then.

Also not shown on any sample schedule is the possibility of adding the piano as accompaniment for a soloist or as part of a chamber music group. Keep this possibility in mind, because many valuable musical experiences are possible using the piano.

In Table 1, each of the twenty-two instrumental classes contains three or more students who may be taught individually or as a class, depending upon how well-matched the players are. Hopefully, some of the classes will be ensembles. Notice that if three individual lessons are given per period, only sixty-six students can be instructed. It is better to resort to alternate-week lessons rather than give individual weekly lessons of ten minutes or less.

At first glance the large number of free periods in Table 2 is puzzling, but those periods can be put to good use. The large classes need careful planning that will occupy much of the free time. Standard procedures such as score study, music library work, and administrative details will take a lot of it also, and the

Table 1				
Miscellaneous Instrument Classes				
Period	Monday	Tuesday	Wednesday	Thursday	Friday
1	Orch.A	Orch.A	Orch.A	Orch.A	Str.Orch.
2	Orch.B	Free	Orch.B	Free	Orch.B
3	Free	Class E	Free	Class N	Free
4	Class A	Class F	Class J	Class O	Class S
5	Class B	Class G	Class K	Class P	Class T
6	Class C	Class H	Class L	Class Q	Class U
7	Class D	Class I	Class M	Class R	Class V

Table 2				
Sectional Rehearsal Classes				
Period	Monday	Tuesday	Wednesday	Thursday	Friday
1	Orch.A	Orch.A	Orch.A	Orch.A	Orch.A
2	Orch.B	Free	Orch.B	Free	Orch.B
3	Free	Free	Free	Free	Free
4	Woodwind A	Woodwind B	Percussion A	Brass A	Brass B
5	Free	Free	Percussion B	Free	Free
6	Strings A	Strings B	Strings C	Strings D	Strings E
7	Free	Free	Free	Free	Free

rest of the unassigned time will be spent coaching individuals as special needs arise. String orchestra is not needed in the schedule of Table 2 because the sectional string classes serve the purpose.

Table 3				
Ensemble Classes				
Period	Monday	Tuesday	Wednesday	Thursday	Friday
1	Orch. A	Orch. A	Orch. A	Orch. A	Str. Orch.
2	Orch. B	Free	Orch. B	Free	Orch. B
3	Free	String Quartet	Free	String Quartet	Free
4	Woodwind Quintet	Bass Quartet	String Quartet	String Quartet	String Quartet
5	Woodwind Quintet	Bass Quartet	String Quartet	String Quartet	String Quartet
6	Woodwind Quintet	String Quartet	String Quartet	Violin Quartet	String Quartet
7	Brass Quintet	Brass Sextet	Percussion	Violin Quartet	String Quartet

The instructional classes shown in Table 3 will contain the following instruments: thirty-two violins; twelve each of violas and cellos; eight string basses; five percussion instruments; five horns; four trumpets; three flutes, oboes, clarinets, and trombones; two bassoons and tubas; one bass clarinet. This schedule is a demanding one that provides for the instruction of enough players for a full symphony and a small training orchestra. The ninety-five students contacted weekly according to the schedule of Table 3 constitute a full teaching load.

Some small schools require one teacher to handle the whole instrumental program. Table 4 shows how this is possible by using every period of every day. Band B and String Orchestra B are

Table 4

Band, Orchestra, and Ensemble Classes

Period	Monday	Tuesday	Wednesday	Thursday	Friday
1	Band A.	Orch. A	Band A	Orch. A	Str. Orch. A
2	Woodwind Quintet	String Quartet	Flute Quartet	String Quartet	Saxophone Quartet
3	Woodwind Quintet	String Quartet	Clarinet Quartet	String Quartet	Percussion
4	Woodwind Quintet	String Quartet	Clarinet Quartet	String Quartet	Str. Orch. B
5	Woodwind Quintet	String Quartet	Clarinet Quartet	String Quartet	Bass Quartet
6	Brass Sextet	String Quartet	Violin Quartet	String Quartet	Bass Quartet
7	Brass Quintet	Trumpet Quartet	Brass Quintet	Band B	Stage Band

preparatory groups. The band and orchestra members instructed would comprise the following instrumentation: eight flutes, four each of oboes and bassoons, fifteen clarinets and one bass clarinet, two alto saxes, one tenor and one baritone sax, six horns, ten trumpets, four trombones, three tubas, five percussion, twenty-four violins, ten violas and cellos, and eight basses. If the school has one hundred and sixteen people enrolled in instrumental music, there is a place provided for their instruction on the schedule of Table 4. It is a herculean task to follow this schedule, and though it has undesirable features—band and orchestra do not meet frequently enough, there is no unassigned time, there are too many lessons to prepare—the strong feature is that all students receive instruction in small groups.

Alternate solutions to the scheduling problem of the school having one instructor can be found by adapting the schedules of Table 1 or Table 2. Band would have to take the place of Orchestra B. The disadvantages of either of these adaptations would be the lack of the possibility of using some of the same personnel in band and orchestra, the filling of the free time by the addition of the band members to the instructional classes, and the large classes that would result.

The string bass quartet

The unusual chamber music group listed as the bass quartet in the schedules of Tables 3 and 4 was advocated by the late Fred Zimmerman of the New York Philharmonic as excellent training for the young bass player. It puts him on his own as he never is in most music, and it gives him the opportunity to play parts of the music texture other than the lowest in pitch. This experience all over the instrument satisfies the musical appetite of the bass player for the singing lines which are so often denied the bass in our school orchestra music. The dearth of literature for the bass is a drawback, but the time spent in transcribing a work is repaid by the extremely mellow harmonies evoked. To make a good arrangement, keep the first part well up on the G string (the thumb and fingers 1, 2, and 3 are usable there), and avoid close spacing of chords built on notes below the D string. If you can make or buy some of these arrangements, by all means schedule a string bass quartet.

The rotating schedule

The schedules of Tables 2, 3, and 4 require rotation so that individuals miss different academic classes each week to receive instrumental instruction. The institution of a rotating schedule meets with much opposition that usually disappears within a few months. The parent and the student are usually willing to let these few classes be missed, since they recognize that it is a sacrifice that must be made in order to get the free instruction. Everyone concerned will agree that a planned absence of one class every six weeks (assuming the rotating schedule operates over six periods) cannot delay a student's progress in school nearly as much as a slight illness that causes him to miss seven classes each day he is out of school. Students manage to make up a week's work missed due to illness within a few days after their return to school. Making up one period each week is not at all difficult, especially because the student is in school that day and can confer with the teacher of the subject missed.

If you want to institute the rotating schedule, you must first convince the administration of the improved program and instruction that will result. You can then gain cooperation of teachers, parents, and students by: (1) explaining that each student will miss only one out of every thirty-six classes—a total of only six classes all year—in any one subject, (2) agreeing to permit students to play in the orchestra without instruction from you if they obtain private instruction on their instrument, (3) agreeing to permit students to go to class instead of musical instruction when the subject teacher deems it especially advisable.

Copies of the rotating schedule must be in the hands of all teachers and office personnel. Students can be provided with a copy, and some should be posted in the rehearsal room. The first of the four pages describes the operation of the schedule, the second contains the names of the students placed in their groups, the third page is a calendar of the school year with the period for each group's lesson marked opposite the date, and page four is a stationary schedule indicating individual practice periods. An example of each of the four pages can be found in Tables 5, 6, 7, and 8.

Table 5

Rotating Schedule, Page One

Instrumental Music Schedule 19__ - 19 __

On the following pages is the schedule of lessons to be given this year. The rotating schedule will be in operation during periods 2 through 7 each day. The rotation takes place in this manner:

The first week of operation, Sept. 30 - Oct. 4, Group A takes a lesson during second period, Group B during third period, etc. The second week, Oct. 7 - 11, Group F takes a lesson second period, Group A third period, etc. Through this system the student misses the same class only once every six weeks, or a total of only six during the entire year.

By using the attached schedule students and teachers can figure when any particular person has a lesson. On page two the person's name appears under the day of the week in a group lettered A,B,C,D,E, or F. On page three the date can be matched to the column of this group to find the period of the lesson.

Students are expected to attend all lessons, except in the case of a dire emergency. Should the instrumental music teacher be absent, the students will report to their regularly scheduled class. Students must fulfill their academic responsibilities, regardless of their absence from class this one period. Teachers are asked to make the same provisions for the making-up of missed work as they would for a student who has been absent due to illness.

A stationary schedule of practice periods for certain pupils during their study periods is attached as page four. These people will report for practice as indicated instead of their regular study period. Study period teachers, please change your study period class lists accordingly.

See me if there are any questions.

(Signed) _____

Instrumental Music Teacher

Table 6

Rotating Schedule, Page Two

Rotating Groups 19 ___ - 19 ___

Group	Monday	Tuesday	Wednesday	Thursday	Friday
A	A.Lass	M.Murawskyj	S.Driver	V.Johnson	R.Larkin
	J.Bland	L.Montes	R.Venanzi	F.Harker	E.Papp
	J.Van Aken	P.Kriegner	M.Bombara	D.Larkin	A.Loewenstein
	K.Callahan	B.Linthicum	D.Case	J.Snelson	A.Bone
B	S.Capozzi	B.Coleman	K.Scheirer	J.Harvey	D.Storey
	R.Angelini	D.DiFrancis	M.Schwartz	E.Burton	D.Tashjian
	F.Viteritto	G.Steward	S.Bartlett	D.McGraw	J.Pitts
	J.Clugston	R.Pietrzak	F.Fishman	W.Montes	I.Floyd
	H.Tarnecky	C.Comiskey	D.Balogh		
C	J.Angelini	S.Alfano	N.Brossoie	D.Marcks	J.Scheirer
	T.Colletti	R.Ryan	L.Felton	N.Sorgler	I.Hirsch
	M.J.Colletti	T.Eckert	E.Jones	K.Krablin	E.Hutchinson
	C.Foulke	K.Morton	W.Holcombe	W.Marlatt	J.Ziegler
D	F.Van Aken	G.Davis	P.Gusz	D.Acquaviva	M.Salange
	S.Gamo	D.Sanders	K.Platt	G.Brennfleck	P.San Paulo
	J.Knosky	F.Stepp	B.Dejnozka	J.Brennfleck	H.Friedman
	P.Morton	D.Perry	J.Barber	J.Wilson	W.Walter
E	S.Weinstein	J.Dickson	K.McElroy	L.Cardozza	S.Hawkyard
	D.Kemo	L.Fletcher	W.Selzer	M.Bondi	S.Brenna
	J.Gross	J.Boogher	S.Morris	J.Pratt	C.Byrnes
	J.Brossoie	G.Lanzi	G.Willoughby	L.Coulton	L.Quinlan
F	(Free)	(Free)	(Free)	(Free)	(Free)

Table 7

Rotating Schedule, Page Three

Rotating Schedule of Music Lessons
Entire School Year 19___ - ___

Directions: Find the date. Look under the column
for your group. The number opposite the date under your
group is the period you come for a lesson. Notify your
regular class teacher each time. A dash instead of a
date indicates there is no school that day.

Date .Group	A	B	C	D	E	F
Sept. 30, Oct. 1,2,3,4	2	3	4	5	6	7
Oct. 7,8,9,10,11	3	4	5	6	7	2
Oct. 14,15,16,17,18	4	5	6	7	2	3
Oct. 21,22,23,24,25	5	6	7	2	3	4
Oct. 28,29,30,31, Nov. 1	6	7	2	3	4	5
Nov. 4,5,6,7,8	7	2	3	4	5	6
Nov. -,12,13,14,15	2	3	4	5	6	7
Nov. 18,19,20,21,22	3	4	5	6	7	2
Nov. 25,26,27,-,-	4	5	6	7	2	3
Dec. 2,3,4,5,6	5	6	7	2	3	4
Dec. 9,10,11,12,13	6	7	2	3	4	5
Dec. 16,17,18,19,20	7	2	3	4	5	6
Jan. -,-,-,2,3	2	3	4	5	6	7
Jan. 6,7,8,9,10	3	4	5	6	7	2
Jan. 13,14,15,16,17	4	5	6	7	2	3
Jan. 20,21,22,23,24	5	6	7	2	3	4
Jan. 27,28,29,30,31	6	7	2	3	4	5
Feb. 3,4,5,6,7	7	2	3	4	5	6
Feb. 10,11,12,13,14	2	3	4	5	6	7
Feb. 17,18,19,20,21	3	4	5	6	7	2
Feb. 24,25,26,27,28	4	5	6	7	2	3
Mar. 3,4,5,6,7	5	6	7	2	3	4
Mar. 10,11,12,13,14	6	7	2	3	4	5
Mar. 17,18,19,20,21	7	2	3	4	5	6
Mar. 24,25,26,27,28	2	3	4	5	6	7
Mar. 31, Apr. 1,2,3,-	3	4	5	6	7	2
Apr. 14,15,16,17,18	4	5	6	7	2	3
Apr. 21,22,23,24,25	5	6	7	2	3	4
Apr. 28,29,30, May 1,2	6	7	2	3	4	5
May 5,6,7,8,9	7	2	3	4	5	6
May 12,13,14,15,16	2	3	4	5	6	7
May 19,20,21,22,23	3	4	5	6	7	2
May 26,27,28,29,-	4	5	6	7	2	3
June 2,3,4,5,6	5	6	7	2	3	4

Table 8

Rotating Schedule, Page Four

Stationary Schedule of Practice Periods

Period	Monday	Tuesday	Wednesday	Thursday	Friday
1					
2		G. Davis F. Stepp		G.Davis F.Stepp	
3	D.Sanders I.Floyd	J. Ziegler J. Brossoie	D. Sanders I. Floyd	L.Quinlan J.Brossoie	L.Quinlan J.Ziegler
4	G. Willoughby D. Balogh	G. Willoughby T. Colletti	A. Bone D. Balogh	A.Bone T.Colletti	R.Zarren
5	J.D'Annunzio M.J.Colletti	J. Angelini L. Montes	J. Knosky M.J.Coletti	L.Montes J.Angelini	J.Knosky H.Tarnecky
6	C.Foulke M.Murawskyj	F. Van Aken P. Kriegner	C. Foulke M.Murawskyj	F.Van Aken P.Kriegner	S.Gamo G.Eldridge
7	B.Holcombe K.Morton	B. Linthicum	B. Holcombe K. Morton	B.Linthicum	

3 SELECTING THE MUSIC

The education a student derives from orchestra depends to a large extent on the music used. For this reason it is a good idea to plan a year in advance to make sure a well-rounded selection of orchestrations will be on hand. In this way you can be sure that different periods of music history will be represented and that there will be a balance between heavy works, light classics, and popular music.

One way to make the education we offer more relevant is to choose music for our school players that they are likely to hear again and again in adult life. The old war horses of music are fresh to young people and surely will be recorded and presented in concerts for yet another generation. These numbers are the ones we are most familiar with, and we can do a good job of teaching them, even though they may no longer appeal to us as musical fare.

More interesting to us will be newer works and the works of lesser-known past composers. Students who are just discovering the beauty of tertian harmony will have difficulty adjusting to new music, but this part of their education is preparation for the future. We must teach it well to prevent the perpetuation of the idea that no valuable music has been composed in the last fifty years. Another mistaken idea we have an obligation to correct is that only the famous composers wrote music that is worthy of performance today. The three B's, Handel, Tchaikovsky, Debussy, Haydn, and Mozart can be supplanted frequently with no loss to the students' musical education.

Much can be taught about musical performance in selections from Broadway shows and orchestrations of popular songs. It is also a relaxing change in rehearsals to play music that is less complicated and gives the whole orchestra a chance to play.

Preliminary selection

The first procedure in choosing ideal music is to decide what compositions you would like to use. Materials available to help you are: (1) catalogs of recordings, (2) reviews and advertisements in periodicals, (3) your personal file of all performances you see, present, and take part in, (4) catalogs of publishers and music dealers. After a list of many compositions is made, selection becomes a process of elimination.

Many compositions in all categories should be put on the preliminary list. Usable as program material are: overtures, movements from symphonies, tone poems, suites, ballet excerpts, selections from musical shows, short classics, light classics, novelties, solos or concerto movements, orchestrations of piano works, orchestrations of popular songs, waltzes, marches, Latin-American dances, patriotic selections, seasonal selections, short modern works, and commissioned works.

Factors to be considered as you evaluate numbers from this list are: (1) the students' instrumental education, (2) the students' education in musical appreciation, (3) the rewarding musical experience needed by each student, (4) the enjoyment desired by the audience, (5) the education that can be given to the audience, (6) your own musical preference. In addition, the music must stay within the limitations of the group, the conductor, the audience, and the time within which the students will have to learn the music. Despite the vast literature of the orchestra, finding a program to fit all the above criteria is difficult.

Final selection

Keeping in mind the categories that are weak in your present library, you can use your budget to acquire the selections that will serve the overall needs. Choose from your preliminary list and retain the rest of the list for reference in future years.

Shopping for music from a catalog can be misleading. Some dealers will provide you with sample scores of the numbers you are considering. Since there may be five different arrangements of one piece, it is advantageous to examine scores in order to obtain the one that fits your group best. An alternate procedure is to secure a return privilege for music that doesn't fulfill your expectations.

The difficulty factor

Assuming a piece of music fits your requirements in terms of being good literature and possible program material, the next most important consideration is the complexity of the problems it will present to you and your players. A professional conductor has his days relatively free to devote to learning his scores well enough to be able to give cues, balance parts, detect mistakes, etc. A school conductor has so many teaching duties that he must avoid compositions that will require more preparation time than he has. He must also realize that his teaching time is limited.

Isolating the cause of difficulty may help you decide whether to buy a certain piece. Rhythmic complexity uses much teaching time in explaining, marking music, and drilling. Range difficulties require much patience until the notes are under control. Passages demanding technical facility can be drilled progressively faster if time permits. Extremes of tempo take much time to develop; fast tempos must be brought up gradually and slow ones brought down. Harmonic complexities can be worked out by adding one part at a time. A work that contains several of these difficulties is likely to require more rehearsal time than one piece warrants.

This is not to say that difficulties should be avoided. An orchestra will rebel at playing music the members consider too easy. They want a challenge, and working on harder music is good for developing their technique. In the final weeks before a performance, deletions can be made if necessary. Notes, sections, or even whole movements can be left out in order to leave rehearsal time for the parts that need to be polished.

Some professional musicians would advise us to use only music of the classic period with school groups in order to avoid technical problems that young players are not equipped to handle. This doesn't work, because there are difficulties present in music that are not inherent in the notes. Haydn and Mozart wrote much music that is technically easy, but it is hard for young people to play precisely enough to present a successful performance of works of this type. Teen-agers are such romanticists anyway that they would rather play Tchaikovsky. The remarkable thing is that mistakes are more tolerable in the fuller textures of the romantic period. All in all, the difficulties of precision in classic music equal the technical difficulties of the romantic, and the school orchestra need not cater to any one period of music history because of the difficulty factor.

School orchestra editions

Publishers have given us special arrangements of masterworks that bypass much problematic material. Some of these editions make only minor changes to lessen requirements of technique and range, yet some change the composition so that it is barely recognizable.

Most masterworks have to be abridged for use with the school orchestra. This is desirable because it reduces the rehearsal time required for one number, thus making it possible to expose the orchestra members to many styles and composers. Some abridged works are not simplified; they are edited with bowings, and parts are cross-cued, but they contain the original difficulties. Others are completely reorchestrated in an attempt to make a better-sounding result possible.

You must examine an abridged edition to determine its suitability for your students. Various methods are used to shorten works. One favorite method is to put the themes together end to end with transitional material between them—the same procedure used in presenting selections from Broadway musicals. Another is to take one theme and some of its development. A symphonic movement is sometimes shortened by cutting directly to the coda from the end of the exposition.

To decide if an abridged edition is a musically valid experience for your students, go through the score mentally without recalling the original. This is the same procedure you would use in evaluating a new composition, and a shortened work is in reality new because of the extreme change in musical form.

Standard orchestral literature

Purists refuse to let their high school orchestras read a masterwork in its original form. In English classes students read Shake-speare's works and other unsimplified, unabridged classics, and they deserve to study the creations of famous musicians in orchestra. They can learn to manage selections from the standard repertoire. As the English teacher explains literature by taking it apart sentence by sentence, so must the orchestra director work out the music phrase by phrase.

Old masterworks involve the transposition problem for some instruments. This can be solved by using a new edition that provides parts for the modern instruments; however, using an older edition lets the players come in contact with a problem professionals encounter daily.

Some directors use only the slow movements of famous works. This avoids technical problems, but the problem of endurance occurs. Producing a rich tone throughout a slow movement is exhausting. An orchestra that lacks technique probably also lacks the ability to sustain the expression of a slow movement. A rich tone is necessary; merely producing the notes is not really playing the piece.

Despite the problems, slow movements can be used successfully with school orchestras. Shorter slow movements will meet with more success, and it is probably a good idea to make cuts in longer ones. Careful rehearsal a few minutes each day develops the endurance and tone.

Fast movements of standard works offer a challenge that is more tangible to the young players. They will be motivated to develop more technique as they see the need for it. For this reason alone, fast movements should be included in programs as often as slow ones.

High school orchestras should have a chance at some of the standard repertoire each year. If they cannot perform a work publicly, reasons for its unacceptability should be discussed at length to impress upon the orchestra the fine points of musical interpretation. Even though a masterwork is not programmed, it serves the educational purpose.

Non-orchestral literature

Chamber music, lesson material, and solos for all instruments belong in the school music library.

Chamber music is available for almost any ensemble, but the

standard ones are: string quartet, violin quartet, duos, trio sonatas, solos with string accompaniment, brass quintet, and woodwind quintet. Cello ensembles and bass ensembles provide special incentives for players of these larger instruments. Some works for small orchestra might be called chamber music, and some of these should find their way into your programs. String orchestra music must also be a standard part of the library, though it fits the definition of chamber music only if there is one player to a part. Buying a 1-1-1-1-1 set for a string orchestra piece is an economical way of trying it out with your students. If it is too easy or too difficult for your string orchestra, you can still use it as chamber music.

Percussion ensembles lack a standard instrumentation, but modern composers are fond of writing chamber music for the percussion instruments. The variety of tone color in the various instruments gives interesting possibilities. Traditionally unimportant percussion parts prevent a percussionist from developing the musicianship he can learn as a member of a percussion ensemble.

Lesson material must be available for all the groups and individuals that you teach. Your teaching will be more efficient if you use books with which you are familiar. Later, supplementary material can be worked into your regular course of study. Select material that complements what is being used; choose a new book that uses a different approach from the ones you have.

Your basic method book should provide for improving the technique of each player. The scale and articulation exercises of Pares have been transcribed for all instruments, and they are available for use with any group. Fussell's *Ensemble Drill*[1] contains many years' worth of study material in one book that can be used with any ensemble; for developing the technique of high school players this book is highly recommended.

Books for special instruction of the different instruments should be examined. Their content varies from all Pares-type studies to all solos. The lesson material chosen should provide exercises for the development of technique, tone, rhythm, phrasing, and intonation. Since no one book does this, select new books that emphasize areas in which your present books are weak.

---

[1] Raymond C. Fussell, *Exercises in Ensemble Drill*, Second revised edition (Minneapolis, Minn.: Schmitt, Hall, & McCreary Company, 1962).

Many solos with piano accompaniment should be on hand. Difficult ones can be used for study purposes, but for performance purposes choose solos that do not overly challenge the students' capabilities; stage fright has a way of keeping a student from doing his best. Once a student has learned a solo, the orchestral accompaniment can be rented. Accompaniments bought for one performance might never be used again.

The economic factor

No matter what the size of your music budget, it would be easy to spend it all on orchestrations. Chamber music, lesson materials, solos, and string orchestra musn't be neglected, however.

Because of ever-increasing prices, it is impractical to discuss here what a budget should be, but it is easy to figure your needs by taking into account your present library, your performance requirements, and the number of students you must instruct.

Your present library can be drawn upon for numbers that you have not used previously with students who will be in your orchestra. If you have a three-year school, numbers from programs of the last two years are unusable for the coming year. Excluding these numbers, there should be a cushion of at least one year's program material in reserve. If new numbers prove unsuited to your group, old ones can be drawn from the cushion.

Performance requirements determine how many selections you need to buy each year. Buy the music for a year even if you plan to use some old numbers, and your library will gradually become replete with usable selections of all types of music. To determine the adequacy of your budget for orchestra music, simply figure the cost of the previous year's programs. Look up the price of each number you programmed. Use a new catalog so that rises in price will be taken into account. Add thirty per cent to this figure if your library is less than three years old, or if it doesn't provide enough string parts for your incoming orchestra.

Though each student will not need a new instrumental method book each year, the budget for method books can be figured on this basis so that some other books can be purchased to supplement the usual technique books. The expenditure per pupil for method books will approximate what is spent on texts in other areas.

Solo and chamber music literature should be part of every student's experience. This means an investment to provide a solo for every student and a piece of chamber music for every four. The expenditure for solos can be cut down by buying collections and unbinding the solo book. In this way a few students can study from the same book.

See Table 9 for a sample music budget.

Ordering music

You will have a well-rounded folio of music for the year if you use the following steps in acquiring new pieces.

1. Make a large preliminary list of numbers you would like to use. Include music of all categories: overtures, suites, symphonies, popular, novelties, patriotic, modern, seasonal, etc. Provide for string orchestra, chamber ensembles, soloists, and other small groups you intend to have.
2. If possible, examine twice as many scores from your preliminary list as you are able to purchase. Eliminate works that you find unsuitable.
3. Order selections from all categories representing several periods of music history. Provide enough copies for your strings and order full scores if they are published.
4. Keep the list of unordered numbers for future reference.

Table 9

Sample Music Budget

$ 150   per program (average)

<u> x 4</u>   programs per year

$ 600   per year budget needed for orchestra music

$ 1.25 per method book

<u> x 100</u> students to be instructed

$125.00 method book budget required

$ 1.00 per solo (average)

<u> x 100</u> students

$100.00 solo music budget

$ 2.50 per piece of chamber music

<u>   x 25</u> chamber groups

$ 62.50 chamber music budget

$600.00 orchestra music

 125.00 method books

 100.00 solos

<u> 62.50</u> chamber music

$887.50 total music budget

4 ORGANIZING THE ORCHESTRA

The final musical results depend upon what takes place in rehearsals. Imagine what results would be obtained in the following example of the first rehearsal of the "Exville High School Orchestra."

Tuning is called for, but the oboe and bassoon reeds won't play and the piano is a quarter-tone flat. The tympanist can't find his pitch pipe, so a clarinet sounds the tuning note.

Ten tuning pegs are stuck, three bows won't tighten, and the bass bows make no sound because they need rosin, which no one can find.

Everyone chose his own seat, and some sections are split, which the director notices as he weaves through the orchestra passing out music. There aren't enough parts, so some violinists must sit three at a stand. The first trumpet player is relieved that his part has been lost, because his valves are stuck and he has no oil.

Nonetheless, the conductor gives a downbeat, and the orchestra starts to play. The first clarinet part is loud with three people playing it, and there is plenty of bass with the anxious tuba player reading over the shoulder of a string bassist.

The conductor wants a fresh start at measure 72, but the orchestra parts have rehearsal letters instead of measure numbers. They start again from the beginning and play to the same point where the conductor insists the horns should not be playing. A short walk to the back of the orchestra proves fruitful when it is discovered that the horn parts are from a different arrangement.

While the right parts are being located, the conductor asks everybody to count from the beginning to find measure 72 and mark it, but no one has a pencil. The bell rings in the middle of his sentence about good musicians always having a pencil, and the orchestra, relieved that the first rehearsal is over, departs, while the conductor goes to find a pencil to mark letter A in his score.

The need for organization

The example of "Exville" shows what a lack of organization can do to a rehearsal. "Exville's" orchestra director relies on the stimulus of the incoming students to get him thinking about what must go on that period. The reason his first rehearsal (and probably many more to come) has been wasted is that he didn't do the preliminary work necessary for a successful rehearsal to take place.

Planning is the first step toward a productive rehearsal; the needs of the orchestra and conductor must be anticipated. In other words, what do you want to do, and what do you and your players need in order to accomplish it? These needs must be provided for in advance of the rehearsal. The time saved is sure to make the final musical results better.

Rehearsal time is saved by the director who is willing to spend time organizing the orchestra. Over a span of a few years you can implement methods that will make rehearsal time free of details that do not bear directly on the music. Once begun, good organization is not difficult to maintain.

The first rehearsal

Under some conditions the first rehearsal must be an organizational meeting. It is better to have this rather than a haphazard attempt at music making that may sour the students on orchestra. Before the orchestra can function, the members must know where you expect them to sit and which part they are to play. This can be covered in the organizational meeting along with the rules and regulations you expect students to obey, what discipline you expect, and what effort you expect to be put forth. Also give them something to look forward to, such as special projects, trips, or music to be undertaken. Try to explain in words what they will gain from orchestra membership. Plan the meeting thoroughly so that you don't have to grope for words. If you run out of things to say, let the orchestra members study for the rest of the period. Before they go, remind them to have their instrument ready to play for the first music rehearsal.

Below are steps you can take to assure the smooth operation of the first music rehearsal of the year.

1. Check all stringed instruments for adjustment long enough before the first rehearsal to allow time for corrective work to be done.
2. Put the music to be rehearsed in the folio beforehand. Check to see that rehearsal numbers agree with your score. If not, change your score to agree with the parts. Before the first rehearsal replace parts that have been lost.
3. Use a broad-point, felt-tipped pen to make placards with members' names and the parts they are to play on them. Place each person's card on his chair.
4. Attach a pencil to each music stand or place one in each folio.
5. Provide well-soaked, tested stock reeds for double-reed players unless they are very experienced in reed maintenance. Use a tuning bar or electronic tuner to sound the A.
6. Have some oil, reeds, rosin, and spare bows on reserve in a handy place.
7. See that the percussion cabinet contains the instruments called for in the scores to be rehearsed.

Seating

If your orchestra lacks a full instrumentation, you will want to experiment with the seating to get the most balanced sound possible. Acoustical factors that affect seating are:

1. Sound from players on the edge of the stage, in front of the curtain line, will project more than that of those behind.
2. If an acoustical shell is used, sound projection of the players close to it will be greater.
3. Sound from players on risers projects better.

The three points just mentioned sound like advantages, but wind players in these positions can easily overpower a small string section. Other acoustical factors should also be taken into consideration:

4. The trumpet and trombone sound is very directional; sometimes it is best to have the bells pointed across the stage instead of toward the audience. For the same reason an upright bell for the tuba is desirable.

5. Almost all the sound of a stringed instrument comes from the top of it; the listener who sees the F holes will hear the full sound of the instrument.

Orchestral tradition places players together in a type of chamber music grouping in order to help them play together. Principles derived from this tradition are:

1. The first row of strings around the conductor is a string octet: two firsts, two seconds, two violas, and two cellos, with the firsts on the conductor's left.

2. The middle of the woodwind section will be a woodwind quartet: first flute, first oboe, first clarinet, and first bassoon, with the first horn also near.

3. Basses are placed directly behind the cellos because of the many passages they play together.

4. The rhythmic center of the orchestra, the percussion, should be close to the physical center. Remember that most of the sound of the bass drum comes from the side that is struck.

An unusual stage or an unbalanced instrumentation may require an unusual seating for best results, but experiments in seating that go against the aforementioned principles should be tried on a large amount of music before permanent changes are made.

Auditions for seating

Within each section you will want the best player in the first seat. Most players will vie for the prestige of this place, and frequent auditions for it will give everyone an incentive to work and keep working.

Thorough auditions using many selections can be scheduled. This type of audition takes much time. Tape record the performances so you can check your decisions. Perhaps you will want a third party to listen to any that you're in doubt about. Using a student for this is a questionable procedure. A lack of a thorough musical background makes a student unable to decide between two good players, even if he can be impartial.

Spontaneous auditions take little time, and they teach players something about performance. Also, each player will keep working hard if he knows he may be asked to play alone while the others listen. Choose a spot for this that is difficult, but avoid embarrassing everyone by asking individuals to play something that none of them can manage.

Music management

The mechanics of keeping track of the music should be arranged so that loss of any parts will be detected. This encourages students to take good care of their parts; they will want to avoid having to pay for lost or damaged ones.

Each piece of music must be labeled in ink with the folio number into which it goes, so that parts will not be switched from one folio to another. Label violin parts I-1, I-2, etc.; II-1, II-2, etc. If your budget will allow, furnish each player with a part. Then he has no excuse for not practicing, and he will have to pay for any sheet of music that does not appear with his number on it at the end of the year. In other words, students don't share textbooks in other classes, and neither should they share folios in orchestra.

In distributing music, make sure every folio has every piece of music in it. Mark the folio number on each sheet of music before passing it out. In case some folios are not present when a certain piece is distributed, you will know by the number exactly in which folio each sheet of music belongs. Use a place marker for unpublished parts listing the name of the composition, the instrument, the folio number, and instructions stating what the player should do during that number (share a part, remain tacit, etc.).

Keeping records

Placing facts in booklets or folders can use up days of a teacher's time. In an attempt to be perfectly organized, you may decide to keep many records of your orchestra members and their activities. Before you start a procedure of keeping a certain type of record, ask yourself, "Will someone ever want to look up these facts I'm planning to set down?" If the answer is no, don't bother; your time is needed elsewhere.

One item that will keep your personnel records complete is a folder for each student that is used much as the folders in a doctor's office, for keeping track of the experiences the student has had. In this folder you can keep records passed on to you from former teachers, music aptitude test results, written theory test papers, records of completed instruction books, lists of solos studied, descriptions of instrumental activities in and out of school, names and phone numbers of private teachers, contracts for the use of school instruments, parents' name, and the make, model, and serial number of his instrument. Many of the above records can be kept easily by using a pre-made form that requires only a mark here and there to make it useful.

An inventory of running supplies can be set up on standard forms. List everything that you ever might want to order. Taking inventory will tell you whether you need a certain item, and a check mark will be enough of a reminder for you to order it.

Many uses can be found for a mimeographed form listing all orchestral instruments down the left side. It can be used for instrument inventory, a check list for missing music, a help in planning seating, a reminder of instruments that need to be repaired, etc. Run a line across the page under the name of each instrument, and you will have room to the right to fill in the necessary information.

Student aides

Many of the mechanical, time-consuming tasks that have to be done could be done by students, as mentioned in Chapter II. Sometimes it is easier to do something yourself than it is to explain to somebody what to do, but students can be a great help in a repetitive process that involves no decision-making on their part. Stamping dates on forms and making lists of music or personnel are tasks that anyone can do. With a little instruction, students can fill out music library forms, file music, help take inventory, make copies, edit music, clean instruments, and do other such projects. Artistic students can make visual aids for you.

To make good use of student help, you must plan their work ahead of time. Instead of using a whole period of your time doing a chore, spend a few minutes setting up the work so that a student can do it later.

Schedule only one helper at a time if he will have to work unsupervised. Take time to explain the task thoroughly, and watch him go through the operation a few times. If you will be supervising, schedule a group of aides. Large amounts of work can be accomplished during these periods.

The lesson plan book

A great aid to an organized program is the lesson plan book. Use it to provide reminders of work you want to do. Include plans for the use of your unassigned time. Write down each task you intend to perform.

In describing lessons you are going to give, include skills to be drilled, instruction to be given, assignments to be made, and music to be rehearsed. The best time to plan the next lesson is at the end of the lesson the students are leaving. This way you are sure that the students are progressing from what they know to what they don't know.

Elsewhere in the plan book write down materials to be ordered, study aids to be made, conferences to be scheduled, field trips to be arranged, and long-range projects to be accomplished. Draw items from these lists to attend to during your unassigned time.

Grading

The grade book is so unimportant to the teacher that he tends to neglect his obligation to keep careful records in it. The student is concerned about his grade since it will appear on his academic record. An organized grading procedure can encourage a student toward a systematic effort to improve his musical skills.

The grade book provides for daily grades for each student which you may or may not feel able to give. At any rate, give as many grades as you can in order to have a sound basis for your awarding of a report card grade. During one lesson a student could be given four or five grades, each based on the different music or the different skills involved. Written assignments and tests give a tangible grade, and some students learn better this way than by verbal explanations.

At the end of a rating period you will feel justified in giving a grade if it is a just appraisal arrived at by averaging the student's work for the whole term. You could probably guess a student's final grade after only a few lessons, but to make sure one bad lesson near the end of a rating period doesn't stick in your memory, give many grades and use them as a basis for the final judgment.

Set up the grade book in the order that you see the students to make your day by day grading easier, even though the transfer to the report cards at the end of the rating period will be difficult. Check off each mark in the grade book as you place it on the report card to avoid missing any.

Editing music

The most time-consuming project you can embark on is marking each person's part to explain how you expect the music to be played. You will seldom find a publication edited as you would like. An edition that contains fewer or different marks than you would like is a problem. Adding or changing editorial marks takes hours.

Having the students mark their parts will save you hours of work, but it wastes precious minutes of rehearsal time, and it is woefully inaccurate. Try a simple experiment having your orchestra members number the measures of a piece of music. You can expect as many as five different locations for measure 100.

The professional method is that markings are made during the first reading of a work. Principal string players are watched, and the bowings they use are marked by the inside player on each stand. The conductor's phrasing and dynamic indications are noted on the part by each wind player the first chance he gets. This method can be adapted to the school orchestra by having the principal string quartet rehearse the music beforehand. See that their parts are edited as you wish. Stop frequently in the full rehearsal to give all players time for marking. Much training will be necessary so they will know what to look for and how to mark it in their part. The first rehearsal of a piece is not the one to use for editing, because the players have so many other things to think about. Once they have a general idea of the piece, a rehearsal can be set aside for the editing.

Thoroughly edited parts will help less-experienced players to learn traditional phrasing. It is worth the time required to prepare at least one piece of music in this fashion that will graphically show the students what types of procedures are used to get musical results. In the process editing marks are taught that the students can use in marking their own parts.

Student aides can help edit music that must be marked, thereby saving rehearsal time. They can copy red-pencil markings the conductor has put in his score, or a sample edited part can be prepared for them to follow. A small group can work quickly and efficiently by marking the music of one particular instrument at a time. Direct supervision is necessary to make sure the marking is uniform and correct.

Rehearsing an unedited section of music thoroughly is an effective means of achieving ensemble without placing a single mark in any part. The phrasing is taught as the music is rehearsed, and multiple repetitions serve to ingrain the proper rendition upon the mind of each player in a way that is even more effective than editing. Indeed, one of the difficulties with edited parts is getting players to observe the markings. Of course, the disadvantage is the rehearsal time required for the multiple repetitions.

Organizing the music library

Adapting usual library procedures will enable you to keep track of all music that the school owns. The minimum requirements are a master list of holdings and a card catalog listing the compositions by title. A card catalog arranged by composer and one arranged by type of composition would be welcome aids in ordering new music and planning programs. A separate catalog of solos and method books by instrument is convenient when searching for appropriate material for an individual student.

Such an elaborate procedure is not necessary when the library is small, but that is the best time to start organizing things the way you want them. Once the library grows to a moderate size, weeks of work will be required to put a system into operation.

The complete list of holdings should be kept in a loose-leaf notebook. Index tabs can divide the notebook into the three sections necessary to list orchestra music, chamber music, and instructional materials for individuals (method books and solos). List present holdings on standard loose-leaf sheets using a separate line for each entry. Simply list a call number, title, and composer. Add the date of purchase and the price if the music is to be insured, in which case a duplicate master list must be kept on file with the staff member in charge of school property insurance.

For listing new acquisitions, copies of music orders can be placed in this notebook, and only the call number need be added. Use the prefix CH for chamber music call numbers and S for solos.

The card catalog of titles is a ready reference. Many things could be listed on each card, but the title, composer, arranger, and call number usually will suffice. Any other information can be obtained by examining the publication itself.

An author catalog card for each selection can be made if you are particularly composer-conscious or if you want to make sure of an adequate representation of all composers in your library. It is a way of checking your holdings from the different periods of music history.

For program planning, a card catalog separating titles according to types of composition is extremely convenient. This corresponds to the subject catalog of a regular library. Simply arrange the cards of all overtures alphabetically behind the "Overture" index card, the novelties behind the "Novelty" card, etc. When the classification of a number is in doubt, put a card in both places. For instance, a Latin-American novelty can be filed as "Latin-American" and also under "Novelty."

Chamber music can be classified in the subject catalog, also. Make index cards for string quartet, brass quintet, violin duos, etc. File the cards by title only or title and composer.

Holdings for each instrument can be filed in the subject catalog. Make an index card for each type of instrument, and file all cards having an S prefix behind the proper card. Remember to make an index card for the general technique books which will also have an S prefix.

The music itself is best placed in a protective envelope or folio and stored in a legal-size filing cabinet. An alternate method is to use boxes especially made for music filing. These can be stored on open shelves. Solos and music for small groups are best placed in a filing cabinet separate from orchestra music.

When an order of music arrives, place a copy of the order in the master notebook. Assign a call number to each piece of music. Place the call number on the protective envelope, box, or cover of each selection. Make a file card for the title (and others for composer, type of selection, and instrument if you wish) including call number, title, composer, and arranger.

Writing the music order

Write separate orders for (1) chamber music, (2) orchestra music, and (3) other music. This way you will be able to use copies of the order sheets as your master list in the notebook, and your needs will be clear to the music dealer, since he may have the title you want in solo, ensemble, and full orchestra versions. Attach a list of your instrumentation to the orchestra music order to be sure of getting an adequate set of parts.

Orchestra music is generally sold in sets according to the string complement. If you desire strings with two each of first and second violins and one each of viola, cello, and bass, order set A. This is indicated as 2-2-1-1-1. 5-5-3-3-3 is set B, and 8-8-5-5-5 is set C. If you want 11-11-7-7-7, order set C plus A to B parts. Set C plus A to C parts would give you 14-14-9-9-9.

Price can be computed from the difference between sets. If you want set C plus A to C parts, the price will be the price of set C plus the difference between the prices of sets A and C. For example, suppose the prices of the three sets of a composition are $10.00, $14.50, and $19.00; set C plus A to C parts would cost $19.00 plus $9.00—$28.00.

Standard orchestral literature is sold with only one of each string part to a set. Each additional string part must be purchased on an extra-part basis whereby no economy can be practiced. Order only what you need, and mark on the title card what parts are with the set. This will remind you to order additional parts if you use the number later with a larger orchestra.

Some older school orchestra music has violin parts labeled "Advanced Violin," "Violin A," "Violin B," "Violin C," and "Second Violin." Violin C is a substitute for viola, and the second violin usually plays along rhythmically with this part, making it like part of a divisi viola section rather than second violin. Violin A is the first violin part restricted to stay within first position. Violin B is the real second violin part, but it is restricted to stay below the notes of Violin A. Advanced Violin is often an octave higher than Violin A.

The set of parts is supplied with advanced, Violin A, and Violin B parts making up the total required number of first violin parts. The viola-like second violin parts will be supplied in the usual number. To use these parts as supplied would result in a divisi first violin section with unison second violins. The best musical result would be obtained by using Violin A for first violins and Violin B for second violin, discarding the rest of the parts. Economically this would be a strain, since all the Violin A and B parts not normally supplied with the set would have to be ordered on an extra-part basis. Depending on the size of your string section, this might make the number more costly than it is worth.

Inventory

Inventories are proofs of loss in case of fire or theft, and the insurance company must have an accurate description of all property involved in a claim. The make, model, serial number, date of purchase, and purchase price should be listed for every piece of valuable equipment. To guard against loss of the inventory, make four copies. File one with the school principal, one with the staff member in charge of school property insurance, and keep two copies for yourself, one to be kept at home and one in school.

While taking inventory at the end of the school year, inspect each instrument to make sure it is in working order. Place a memo in the case describing all malfunctions so the repairman knows where to start looking for the trouble. Note on the inventory sheet which instruments need new cases and which need to be replaced.

Make standard forms for your inventory that can be filled out with check marks. Avoid unnecessary forms such as record cards of each instrument; all information can be kept on the inventory form. Organize well enough to make the orchestra an efficient group with smooth-running performances and rehearsals, but spend the rest of your available time on musical matters.

5 REHEARSAL PROCEDURES

Program preparation and thorough learning of the music are the goals of the rehearsal. Both are accomplished through procedures that help students to develop the understanding necessary to play their part artistically.

Polishing a performance can be a process just as systematic as the polishing of a rough diamond. As each facet of the diamond is brought to shape, so must each musical detail be formed.

Musical phrases can be formed using definite procedures. Adequate planning of the rehearsals provides for the use of these procedures day by day until a program is learned.

Efficient organization shortens the preliminaries so that the main body of the rehearsal is spent in learning the music. Efficient procedures save time also, allowing each passage to be thoroughly learned. Review must be provided to make the learning permanent and insure a successful concert.

Rehearsal format

A set routine to the rehearsal will save time and eliminate unnecessary confusion. Each student will have to know where you expect him to enter the room, place his books, obtain his instrument and music, be seated, assemble his instrument, and place his empty case.

The quickest way to get a rehearsal started is to make each student responsible for his own equipment. The use of librarians to hand out music and instruments will delay the starting time, and it holds no advantage. If each person handles his own instrument, there is no doubt who is at fault if it gets broken. The same applies to lost music.

In an ideal traffic flow pattern, a student would enter near where his instrument is stored, unpack it, and place his books and empty case in the storage compartment. If the instrument storage area is small, he must keep the empty case near his orchestra seat; however, everyone must have a clear passageway in case of a fire drill. When the fire bell rings, players of large instruments must set them down without blocking the way; players of smaller instruments can take their instruments with them.

A rehearsal call board (a section of the chalk board can be used) lets the players know what numbers are to be rehearsed that day. Listing the numbers here lets the players know what special equipment will be needed. Time is saved if mutes and percussion traps are prepared in advance. Also, players who double will be able to find out from the call board if both instruments will be needed.

WARM UP

It is a good idea to have two warm-up periods in each rehearsal, one before and one after tuning. Wind instruments rise in pitch as they get warmer; strings tend to go flat. Group playing while these things are happening is bound to be out of tune.

The first warm-up period is to be left to the individual. It serves to prepare the embouchures of wind instrument players for playing and to bring their instruments to playing temperature. Soft playing with frequent rests is best. During the rests, air can be blown into the instrument to keep warming it. Woodwind players must finger their lowest note to make the air travel completely through the instrument.

String players can use the first warm-up period to play on all four strings, thereby taking out any slack that may be present. Scales used for this also help to prepare the left hand for playing. A good drill for the bow arm is the playing of a series of down-bows, piano, and a series of up-bows, forte.

The second warm-up period follows tuning and serves to accustom the members of the group to playing together. Balance, tone, control of dynamics, phrasing, and refinement of intonation are subjects that can be improved during this group warm up. The goal is to make each player more sensitive to how the sounds he produces relate to the group. Slow, soft chorales or scales permit him to concentrate on this.

TUNING

School orchestras need much more time for tuning than their professional counterparts. Each player needs a chance to hear how his note relates to the tuning note. The tuning A should be sounded for each section of the orchestra: flutes, oboes, clarinets, bassoons, etc. An electronic tuner or tuning bar is best for this. (See Figure 5–1.)

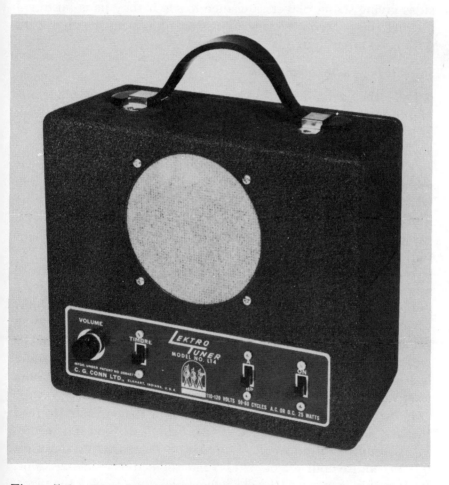

Figure 5–1: THE CONN LEKTROTUNER

The Lektrotuner sounds A or B-flat with a choice of two tone qualities. Photo courtesy of Conn Corporation, Elkhart, Indiana.

A vibraphone is really a complete set of chromatic tuning bars, besides being a musical instrument. If it or a piano is used for tuning, notes other than A are advantageous. All the open string notes can be checked, not only for the strings, but also as a check for the evenness of wind instrument tuning. All the slides of a brass instrument are potential tuning slides. Three of the joints of a clarinet can be manipulated if necessary to provide an even scale.

Even if a keyboard instrument is not used in tuning, time can be taken to have all the E strings sounded, all A strings, etc. Besides giving string players a chance to see if they have mistuned a string, this procedure lets wind instrument players match pitches with notes other than A.

Introducing a new composition

Once the preliminaries of getting ready to play, warming up, and tuning are out of the way, the real work of the rehearsal begins. At the beginning of the year and after the presentation of each program, this time will be spent learning new music.

There are two basic approaches to a composition new to the orchestra: play the whole way through to get a general idea and later work it out part by part, or the opposite—work out each part until the whole piece is learned. Difficulty has a lot to do with deciding which is best. A difficult piece will have to be built phrase by phrase. The *Gestalt*, get-the-whole-idea approach, can only be used on pieces that are easy enough for the orchestra to read through the first time.

Easy pieces need not be limited to the *Gestalt* approach, however; they can proceed from the part to the whole also. Each phrase can be drilled for precision as the work begins. When the end is reached, the piece is pretty well learned. This procedure is especially good for the first music rehearsal of the year to insure a satisfactory experience for all new members.

Even though a piece isn't easy enough for the orchestra to read through, it can be approached by the *Gestalt* method if a recording is used to introduce it. A recording demonstrates phrasing, tempo, and overall effect. It also has some rote teaching value. Besides this, it presents the challenge of learning to play the piece.

A new number consisting of several movements can be introduced by a different approach to each movement. The slow movement can be learned bit by bit, the first movement introduced by a recording, the third movement played through for the idea of the whole movement, etc. The different approaches keep the work interesting and help to inspire the confidence necessary to master a long piece of music.

A verbal introduction to a composition is best cut short before the first reading. The players are anxious to try the piece, and they are in no way prepared to listen to a lecture about it. Interesting sidelights can be saved for later rehearsals.

Following are the previously described approaches to a new composition detailed step by step. Differences and similarities are readily apparent.

I. *Gestalt* Approach
   A. Explain any unusual notation in the piece.
   B. See that all necessary instruments and accessories are ready.
   C. Demonstrate the first phrase; conduct while you demonstrate.
   D. If there are recurring themes, obtain a passable rendition of them before starting at the beginning.
   E. Play straight through, but stop at a convenient place for a fresh start if many players are confused. Shout rehearsal letters as they come so lost players can find the place.

II. *Gestalt* Approach Using a Recording
   A. Have the recording ready to play before rehearsal starts.
   B. Explain any unusual notation.
   C. Stress the need for silence so all parts can be heard when the recording plays.
   D. Stress the need to watch the music carefully to see which notes are played short and which full value, which marcato and which legato, and other details of phrasing.
   E. Conduct while the recording plays, giving cues as though your orchestra were performing. Call out rehearsal letters to make sure everyone has the place.
   F. Let your orchestra try the number. Follow the steps of the regular *Gestalt* approach.

III.   Part-to-Whole Approach
   A.   Explain any unusual notation in the first section of
        the piece.
   B.   See that accessories and instruments used in the first
        section are ready.
   C.   Try the first phrase.
   D.   Stop. Make necessary corrections.
   E.   Play again and try second phrase.
   F.   Stop. Correct second phrase if necessary.
   G.   Play from the beginning and try the third phrase, etc.
   H.   Work on the second part of the composition in the
        same manner. This could be postponed to another
        day if necessary.

Planning the rehearsal.

Once the compositions have been introduced, further work on
them must be planned. Planned rehearsals serve as a map showing the route to a successful concert. The plan can be anything
from a simple notation of what numbers are to be rehearsed to a
complete script of everything that will be said and done during
the rehearsal.

A director who has planned the details he wants to correct will
not have to leaf through his score repeatedly in search of an objective to accomplish. Neither will he have the orchestra play one
number after another from beginning to end without stopping.
He will have planned in advance the work that will take place and
the methods he will use to get the desired results from his players.

Some directors carry every lesson plan in their heads, never
making a notation of any kind. This is fine if you can do it, but if
you try it and find yourself proceeding aimlessly through your rehearsals, a written lesson plan may very well be the best step you
ever took.

Whether the lesson plan is written or not, all good ones include
for each rehearsal: (1) specific music to be improved, (2) specific
objectives to be accomplished with the music, (3) a definite
sequence of activities the teacher will perform, (4) a definite sequence of activities the students will be asked to perform, and
(5) any teaching aids that will be used in the rehearsal.

A typical lesson plan contains several numbers to be rehearsed and one to be reviewed. Following are steps you can use in developing a lesson of this type.

1. Determine what music will be included in the rehearsal. Examine your scores and/or listen to tapes of previous rehearsals to decide what work needs to be done.
2. Pick sections of a few numbers that need much improvement, and choose one number for review that needs only general improvement.
3. Study this music extensively to determine exactly how you want it to be played.
4. Plan techniques of obtaining the desired results from your players.
5. Prepare any special aids you will need.
6. Write the lesson plan, naming each composition and the rehearsal letter at which you want to start.
7. Write down reminders for procedures you plan to use.

Following is a sample lesson plan. For the sake of brevity, the eight compositions of a typical program will be referred to by number in this chapter.

Sample lesson plan

MUSIC TO BE REHEARSED AND SPECIFIC OBJECTIVES:

1. Composition No. 2 from A to B; correct faulty performance of triplet figure.
2. Composition No. 6 from E to the end: teach the theme in its augmented form.
3. Composition No. 1: review.

AIDS TO BE PREPARED:

1. Chart showing a triplet.
2. Chart showing two sixteenth notes followed by an eighth.
3. Chart showing the rhythm of the theme of composition No. 6.
4. Chart showing the same theme in augmentation.

PROCEDURE:

Composition no. 2:

1. Explain the difference between charts 1 and 2.
2. Rehearse both rhythms using concert A; chart 2 first, then chart 1.
3. Drill the triplets between A and B progressively faster.
4. Drill the full orchestra from A to B progressively faster.

Composition no. 6:

1. Explain the compositional device of augmentation using charts 3 and 4.
2. Play the theme regularly.
3. Play the theme in augmentation.
4. Explain the more grandiose character of the augmented theme.
5. Rehearse the orchestra from E.

Composition no. 1:

1. Tell of changes to be made from the last playing:
   a. More trumpet at beginning
   b. More vibrato in strings at C
   c. Less volume of accompaniment at D
   d. Slight tempo change at D
   e. Full accents in final two measures
2. Play straight through.
3. Write down the location of any trouble spots that need work.

In the sample lesson the rehearsal is divided into three different types of activity. In the first, students work on a specific difficulty (the triplets). This kind of drill is best done at the beginning of the rehearsal when the players are fresh. The second type of activity involves work more general in nature (the augmented theme). The third type of activity, the review, gives everyone a chance to play. This is a satisfactory ending to the rehearsal, and it serves to reinforce prior learning. Parts still in need of work can be included in a future lesson plan.

Day to day rehearsal planning runs the risk of neglecting some numbers. To insure an equally musical rendition of all numbers on the prospective program, you can establish a rotating list of compositions to be rehearsed. Divide long numbers into parts and make sure each part gets adequate rehearsal. See Table 10 for a sample rotating list of numbers to be rehearsed.

Table 10

Rotating Rehearsal List

Composition	Rehearsal Dates	
No. 3 to letter C	Mon. 3/5	Fri. 3/9
No. 4 letter D to F	Tues. 3/6	Mon. 3/12
No. 5 entire	Wed. 3/7	Tues. 3/13
No. 6 G to end	Thurs. 3/8	Wed. 3/14
No. 3 C to E	Fri. 3/9	Thurs. 3/15
No. 4 F to end	Mon. 3/5	Fri. 3/16
No. 6 to letter G	Tues. 3/6	Mon. 3/12
No. 7 to letter A	Wed. 3/7	Tues. 3/13
No. 8 A to B	Thurs. 3/8	Wed. 3/14

From Table 10 the rehearsal of Monday, March 5 can be seen to include composition no. 3 to letter C and composition no. 4 from F to the end. On Tuesday, March 6, the rehearsal would include composition no. 4 from D to F and composition no. 6 to letter G.

The other part of each rehearsal is a review number. The review list doesn't rotate strictly, but a different number from it is included in each rehearsal. Comparing Table 10 with Table 11, you can see that after a number has been rehearsed in its entirety it is added to the review list. It still occurs on the rehearsal list, however, so further refinements can be made.

Table 11

Review List

Composition	Review Dates		
No. 1	Mon. 3/5	Thurs. 3/8	Tues. 3/13
No. 2		Tues. 3/6	Mon. 3/12
No. 5		Wed. 3/7	Thurs. 3/15
No. 6			Fri. 3/16
No. 4		Fri. 3/9	Wed. 3/14

The advantage of the lists is that all numbers are rehearsed or reviewed at least once during the week. This way the orchestra is in constant touch with all numbers on the program.

The lists can be used flexibly; one number can be substituted for another. Keep a record of what is rehearsed each period and adjust the rotating list accordingly.

After the schedule operates two weeks, the lists for the next two weeks can be made up, keeping in mind the progress that has been made so far. For instance, if composition no. 3 has been rehearsed from the beginning without reaching the goal of letter C, it must then be set up in the next rotating list as composition no. 3 from B to C.

If one number is doing badly, it can be put into the list twice, and it will automatically receive twice as much attention. A number doing well can be moved from the rehearsal list to the review list. If many numbers are doing badly, the program will have to be shortened by omitting some. If all numbers are doing well, more refinements can be made.

EASIER NUMBERS

Spending much rehearsal time on the difficult numbers of a program may result in the easier ones being neglected. They need careful rehearsal also to insure a good performance. A poorly played easy number mars a concert, and an audience will not be sympathetic when mistakes are made in an easy piece. The tone, intonation, and phrasing in easy pieces should be developed to a high degree. Since the notes are not difficult, more attention can be given to these important aspects of playing. Review often to let the players learn to match phrasing, balance dynamics, and perfect the rhythm of these numbers.

ENDINGS

Despite the method of scheduling different sections of each composition for rehearsal each day, it often happens that the orchestra becomes more familiar with the beginnings of numbers than with the endings. The ending is the impression left with an audience, and it deserves special attention. A refreshing change in rehearsal procedure is to start with the ending of a composition and work back to the beginning. Following is a procedure for doing this.

1. Build the last chord, starting with the bass and adding one part at a time.
2. Rehearse the cadence measures for the proper amount of *ritard*.
3. Rehearse the last phrase, including the cadence and last chord.
4. Rehearse the last section, starting at the last rehearsal letter and going through to the end.
5. Keep going back one rehearsal letter and playing to the very end until the beginning is reached.

Working out difficulties

Sometimes you may wonder where to start correcting a poorly played section. Imprecise and erroneous playing results in such a muddy sound that specific mistakes are undetectable. A great help in such a case is a set correctional procedure.

The first task is to take the orchestra apart, listening to only a few instruments at a time. The second task is to combine the instruments until the full orchestra is playing. This not only eliminates mistakes and adds precision to the playing, it gives the musicians a thorough understanding of the structure of the piece.

A typical musical texture has four parts: melody, harmony, countermelody, and rhythm. In rehearsal these must be isolated from each other to enable meaningful drill to take place.

The melody is a good place to start, though you can begin with any part. After hearing the melody alone and making necessary corrections, listen to the harmony parts that have the same rhythm as the melody. Countermelodies can come next, and the rhythmic accompaniment last.

The parts can then be combined. Start in reverse order with the rhythm and the countermelody, then add the melody and harmony. Later rehearse only melody and harmony together, then melody and countermelody, then harmony and rhythm. This way the players learn how their part fits in with the others.

When difficulties persist, the orchestra must be taken apart still more. For instance, if the melody is so filled with errors that correction is impossible, each of the sections playing it must be checked for accuracy.

Following is an example of a thorough rehearsal procedure for a phrase having a typical orchestration.

1. Correct melody only. If this is impossible,
2. Correct first flute and oboe, then add first clarinet, then
   add first trumpet, then first violins. If violins do not
   agree, add them a few at a time instead of all at once.
3. Correct harmony parts. If this is impossible,
4. Correct second flute and oboe, then add second clarinet,
   then second trumpet, then second violins. If violins do
   not agree, add them a few at a time.
5. Correct countermelody. If this is impossible,
6. Correct bassoons, then add trombones, then cellos. If
   cellos do not agree, add them two at a time.
7. Correct the rhythmic accompaniment. If this is impossible,
8. Correct bass, then add French horns, then violas, then
   percussion.
9. Add the rhythm instruments of step 8 to the countermelody of step 6, then add the harmony instruments of
   step 4, and finally the melody instruments of step 2.
10. Drill the instruments of step 8 with those of step 4, then
    those of step 6 with those of step 2, then step 8 with
    step 2, then step 4 with step 6, then
11. Drill the phrase with the full orchestra.

Correcting mistakes

The teaching the conductor does causes a change in the way
the orchestra members play. He can use words, conducting motions, vocal demonstrations, a student's playing, recorded examples, or a combination of these in his teaching.

Demonstrating the correct version is the most direct means to
bring about desired changes in the playing, although simply explaining verbally does work with an advanced group. Use conducting motions with all demonstrations. A correct performance
by a student is an excellent example to use. A recorded example
will be necessary if the passage can't be demonstrated otherwise.

Demonstrating the incorrect version, reiterating what has gone
wrong, is effective only by way of contrast with the correct version. Since the incorrect version should be forgotten as soon as
possible, demonstrate it only once, and follow it immediately with
two or more demonstrations of the correct one.

Once the players make a correction, have them repeat it immediately. If they played it wrong three times, have them play it right five times to erase all memory of their first version.

In short, to correct a wrong rendition: tell the players what has gone wrong; tell them how to correct it; demonstrate the correct version; and have them review it after they've played it right. Contrast the wrong version with the right one if doing so will increase the students' understanding of the musical principle involved.

Stopping and starting

During the work of correcting mistakes there will be many occasions to stop the orchestra. Stopping the music is frustrating to the students. It is less so if you stop at the end of a phrase. Use the time between the making of the mistake and the end of the phrase to plan how you will correct the mistake and where you will start playing again. Of course, if finishing the phrase is wasting time, it shouldn't be done.

Finding a place to start again is sometimes a problem. Extra rehearsal letters help; seldom are enough provided. Even a simple piece should have a letter at the place where each instrument enters, so that if a person misses his cue you won't have to review the whole preceding section. For a complicated piece measure numbers are preferable.

When it becomes necessary to start at a distance from a letter, you can save time by having the orchestra members count with you. Say "Count measures with me after letter C: 1,2,3,4," etc., until you reach the measure you want. Only people with multiple rests will have trouble. Locating the 28th bar of a 32 bar rest is tricky. It is simple if that bar is counted as 28, the next as 29, etc. until 32, the last bar of the rest is reached. Another possibility that would cause confusion would be four measures of music before a 14 bar rest. This is simply counted as 4, 14 is added, and the next measure is the nineteenth. Though these examples may not seem complicated, they would cause so much trouble in rehearsal that the best way would be to start at the nearest rehearsal letter and play to the trouble spot.

Some delay and confusion is unavoidable when starting in the middle of a piece. High notes have to be prepared, the tympanist may have to retune, etc. This confusion will be kept to a minimum if the starting place is the beginning of a musical phrase.

When starting a phrase having pick-up notes, describe them so the people who don't have them will know when to enter. Give all the necessary information. For example, "I'll count three, then the three eighth-note pick-ups will bring us into measure forty."

Saving time in rehearsal

It may sound strange to say that much rehearsal time can be wasted playing music, but such is the case if a phrase has to be repeated over and over because the conducting motions aren't clear. Long explanations and many repetitions won't be necessary if the motions are well-planned and well-executed. In a problematic area the orchestra may not respond the first time, but if the conductor is consistent, if he does the same thing each time, the players will soon figure out their entrance.

Experimenting with conducting motions in front of the orchestra takes time and confuses the players. If you are convinced that the motions you planned are not going to get results with a certain problematic area, stop working on it and develop better motions in private. Practice conducting a score before trying it with the students if it contains any conducting problems at all. You must be perfectly sure what motions you're going to use.

Giving cues saves rehearsal time. Players will rely on the conductor more than their counting for an entrance. Later they get to recognize their entrance spot by sound, but they will always play better with a cue. A word of caution here: it takes much score study and manual practice to give cues as they are needed.

Timesaving habits should be developed by a conductor. Give instructions only once, and the students will learn to listen the first time. Refuse to say "One, two, ready, play," each time you start. Not only will you save time, but the students will learn the significance of the preparatory beat. Listen to a tape recording of a full rehearsal to see if you have developed any habits that waste time.

Keep the lesson plan book handy during rehearsals. When a complicated problem is making no progress, include it in the plan for the lesson of the people involved. The same thing should be done when an individual is having problems. There's no use in having the orchestra listen to a private lesson. A reminder in the plan book will enable you to solve the problem using lesson time instead of rehearsal time.

Rehearse only the music you've studied. It's impossible to shape a performance until you've had time to decide what shape it should take. To be studying your score during rehearsal is wasting rehearsal time.

All of the subjects covered in this chapter contribute to an efficient rehearsal. A good format for the rehearsal lets it get started sooner. Good procedures for warm up and tuning get those essentials done quickly and correctly. Stopping and starting can be done in a way that takes up no more time than necessary. Set procedures for the main work of correcting mistakes and working out difficulties in the music enable it to be accomplished well without taking an excess of rehearsal time. Above all, a well-planned rehearsal will be sure to proceed swiftly with no time wasted.

Review

The three main activities of a rehearsal are: (1) locating difficulties, (2) working them out, and (3) keeping them from recurring. The third activity should be included as a part of every rehearsal.

The experience of playing a piece through is necessary concert preparation. It is also a welcome change from the stopping and starting necessary to work out the problems. Following are things that can be done to get the most out of the review.

1. Before playing, remind players of details that tend to go wrong.
2. Tell them of effects that need to be greater.
3. Play straight through, stopping only if the players are not responding to your signals.
4. Use signals to call for proper balance and phrasing.
5. Use vocal commands to call for corrections that can't be made by hand signals.
6. Mentally take notes of errors that must be eliminated. Write them down before they escape your memory.

A good time to stress the need for alertness to conducting motions is before a review piece. Signals are more efficient than words; it takes a long time to stop the orchestra and explain things such as proper balance. Appropriate signals can bring this about without a moment's delay.

The last few rehearsals before a concert should be concerned mainly with review. Rather continuous playing during these rehearsals shows the students the amount of endurance they will need to play the concert.

The review in these last rehearsals takes other forms than just playing through the concert, however. Transitional sections and those that involve tempo changes must be reviewed again and again. The beginning sections of all the numbers also need this kind of treatment. Beginnings may falter due to the players' nervousness even though rehearsals have been adequate. To counteract this tendency, review the beginnings often so that the players are extra sure of them.

Rehearsal procedures deal with a number from the time it is passed out to the orchestra. These procedures must provide for a good introduction of the number, a thorough working out of all difficulties, and adequate review. A good concert reflects the success of the procedures used in rehearsal.

6 LESSON PROCEDURE

The main purpose of the lesson is to increase the instrumental performance capabilities of each player. As skills are developed and refined, the playing of the orchestra will improve.

Methods for presenting and refining skills can be made more effective by combining traditional procedures with those made possible by modern technology. Systematic application of these methods will produce well-rounded musicians who are equipped to cope with the problems offered in their orchestra music.

Study material used in lessons will include orchestra music, though not to be neglected are exercises for gaining skills and chamber music and solos for the enrichment they offer. Each lesson must be planned to make progress in all areas.

Planning the lesson

The format for a lesson is difficult to express in minutes spent at each activity, and it is even more difficult to stick to it in giving the lesson. Time would be allotted in a typical lesson as follows:

1. Warm up and tuning: 5 minutes
2. Assignments to be heard: 10 minutes
3. Instruction and drill on the new assignment: 15 minutes
4. Instruction and drill on orchestra music: 10 minutes
5. Playing chamber music or solos: 10 minutes

Exceeding the time allotment in one area will cut short the time you can spend on the others, but this can be adjusted in the next lesson.

The content of a lesson is variable, not at all as rigid as the above timed format suggests. There will be periods when you will want to do something entirely different, such as show a film, read chamber music, work on solos, or spend the whole period giving instruction.

Whatever the content of the lesson is to be, reminders written in the plan book are useful. Greatly detailed plans for a lesson are seldom necessary, however. Simply write down the instruction to be given, assignments to be given and heard, skills to be drilled, and the music to be used.

Assignments

Before a student can practice an assignment, he must understand it perfectly. If there are notes or rhythms that are not clear in his mind, he may not be able to figure them out at home. Part of the lesson must be used to explain the assignment fully.

In making an assignment to a group, consider the average player in that group. Some of the players may not have to practice at all to master the assignment; others may not be able to master it. Vary the weekly assignments to emphasize different aspects of playing. Whatever the assignment, drill the class in it so that each member will be able to start work on it with a clear understanding of what he's trying to accomplish.

Whenever possible, the assignment should be an open ended one—one where the student is challenged to increase his proficiency. Technique studies can be assigned this way. Once the class learns to play a scale or study, an assignment is given to learn to play it faster. The talented student is not limited in such an assignment, and the less talented feels no sense of failure as long as he makes some improvement.

An individual or a class that is having problems with a technical detail needs drill on it. It may be impossible to find the right type of material. If so, create your own exercises to serve the purpose. You will be sure the exercises you write will be applicable, and use of them will avoid a long, perhaps futile, search. Many of the exercises advocated in this book are unpublished and will have to be written out if you wish to use them.

Take advantage of the presence of tape recorders in many homes today by assigning students to listen to tapes that you prepare. These recordings may be in the form of canned lessons. A student could easily get the information from a lesson he missed if you were to record it for his later listening. Some students could take two lessons each week, one of them recorded.

Another form of prepared tape would set an example for the student. You could do the playing, have an advanced student do it, or use a solo from a commercial recording.

In the same way, a tape of a student's orchestra part could be made for him to study. In lessons you can only demonstrate a passage so often before you run out of time; the student could listen to a tape of it at home over and over, and you would only have to take time from the lesson for one demonstration.

Instruction and drill

The basic things that the lesson must be concerned with are the elements of instrumental performance. All changes that a player is ever asked to make come under one of five categories: phrasing, rhythm, intonation, tone, or technique—PRITT for short. Students must become familiar with these five areas in lessons and work toward further accomplishment in each.

PRITT training is involved throughout the lesson. Weaknesses in any area should be diagnosed for each player and some remedial exercises prescribed. An instrumentalist's performance is appreciated to the extent that he has mastered the five skills of PRITT. Occasionally, the usual lesson format must be sacrificed to make possible a thorough study of one subject. Students with little knowledge of the PRITT concept would benefit by a complete period of explanation of each element.

These full periods of instruction must be planned in detail. It is a good idea to tape record the presentation. Because of the fundamental importance of this instruction, you will want every student to have it. Those who miss a lesson can hear it on tape.

PHRASING

A complete lesson dwelling on phrasing could be spent on examples from orchestra music. In fact, the orchestra music part of regular lessons is likely to be concerned mainly with phrasing.

Breathing, bowing, tonguing, and all the other processes that affect the ebb and flow of music become more important as the notes come under control.

Exercises in articulation such as those by Pares develop fundamental phrasing skills. Lacking these, you can assign regular scales to be played with a variety of bowing and articulations. Many of these variations can be shown in the lesson on phrasing. For instance, consider the possibilities of the four note group with two slurred and two staccato. On wind instruments the length of the staccato notes must be adjusted to the tempo, and the last of the slurred notes must be cut short enough not to run into the first staccato note. An extreme tempo can be developed at which the short notes have to be double-tongued. On stringed instruments the bowing must be adjusted to the tempo. A very slow tempo would require a whole bow, tip-tip, whole bow, frog-frog bowing. The extreme tempo would call for the whole figure to be played at the frog with the two short notes bouncing, up-up.

Control of dynamics, the production of an accent, the *forte-piano* attack, *marcato* playing, *leggiero* playing are other examples of things that you might choose to include in a lesson on phrasing. The effects that are not successful in orchestra will naturally be the ones you'll want to teach in your phrasing lesson.

RHYTHM

One or more whole lessons can be used to increase the students' ability to deal with basic rhythmic problems. They must know note values perfectly to be sure where the conductor's baton will fall in relation to the notes on their page.

A written test will quickly tell you the extent of their rhythmic understanding. Ditto a page of music containing problems you think your students should be able to solve. Have them mark the beats (and the subdivisions if you wish) of each measure.

There is a gulf between understanding and being able to perform rhythms. This gap can be bridged by slow practice using a tap of the foot as a marker for the beat. The foot is preferable to a metronome at first; the student can disregard the click of the metronome much easier than he can disregard his physical involvement with the beat. Later the foot can be replaced by the metronome and the tempo made faster with each repetition.

The playing of a fugue is a severe test of the ability to perceive and execute rhythms. Fugues exist in many forms, from the fughettas of the early baroque to the masterpieces of J. S. Bach. A fugue that suits the ability of the class can be chosen for study. The lesson will take up one period or part of several as shown in the steps below.

1. Each student marks the beats above each measure in his part.
2. The teacher checks the marking for accuracy.
3. The teacher briefly explains the structure of the fugue being studied.
4. The exposition of the fugue is rehearsed with the teacher conducting.
5. The entire fugue is rehearsed, first with and then without a conductor.

Rhythms that students are having difficulty with in orchestra can be studied in the rhythm lesson. A specially written study provides the drill that is needed. Mix the problematic rhythm with conventional rhythms to make the study more than a drill that could be played by rote. Write in easy keys and keep the notes on the staff.

Students often play the subdivision of the beat wrong by giving a note one-third of a beat when it should get one-half, and vice versa. This mistake and others like it point out the need for exercises drilling on the change between duple and triple subdivisions of the beat. Joseph Paulson has written exercises for this and other rhythmic problems in his folio entitled *Get in Rhythm*.[1]

INTONATION

Intonation may be defined basically as the matching of pitches, but there is more to it than that. Performers playing the same melody must agree in pitch, but also, to be acceptable to you, the pitches of that melody must agree with your idea of what those pitches should be. Your concept of pitch relationships has been shaped by your musical experiences in our culture. When you are

---

[1]Joseph Paulson, *Get in Rhythm* (Westbury, N.Y.: Pro Art Publications, Inc., 1948).

teaching intonation, you are trying to have the students learn this traditional concept of pitch relationships.

Many students reach high school with little knowledge of what intonation is. Wind instrument players tend to depend entirely upon the instrument to produce the required pitch. String players often play out of tune despite their awareness of the process of adjusting the pitch. (This will be discussed more fully in Chapter 8.)

A lesson on intonation is worthwhile for all students because it is something that must be constantly evaluated as a person plays. An out-of-tune player is a weak link in the chain, a drop of mud in the clear water. The intonation lesson clarifies the meaning of the term to each student and provides a basis for improving his skill at playing in tune.

Intonation can be studied systematically from an acoustical approach. First the student learns about the acoustical phenomenon known as beats. Then he learns to eliminate beats that result when he is out of tune with the tuning A. (The volume of the A and the player's note must be the same.) This may be his first experience in consciously matching pitches. After he can do this, he must learn to tune the note on his instrument that is an octave away from the tuning note. Later he learns to play a fourth away from a reference tone without causing beats. Through this procedure he becomes sensitive to how his pitch relates to another that is sounding at the same time.

The second stage of intonation training deals with intervals. The procedure is similar to learning a foreign language by means of a record. An instrument capable of sustaining tones is used for sounding the reference pitches. A melodic interval is played slowly so that the student can join in each note and match pitches with it. The students who learn to tune all intervals exactly will be able to hold their intonation, even in chamber music when they are the only one on the part. Students who have trouble tuning intervals can still contribute to the orchestra if they can match pitches.

Several electronic devices are available to help in teaching intonation. Many teachers scorn these, saying their ear is all they need. It's true that all one needs is a well-trained ear in order to *judge* intonation, but to *teach* it we need all the help that we can get.

Stroboscopic devices offer a sort of programmed learning. The student plays a note into the microphone and the device shows him visually if the note is sharp or flat. (See Figure 6–1.) By using this machine, the student can adjust his instrument even without the aid of a teacher. A more elaborate model of this instrument displays the complete chromatic scale at all times. It is usable by instruments pitched in any key, and it gives readings for seven octaves. (See Figure 6–2.)

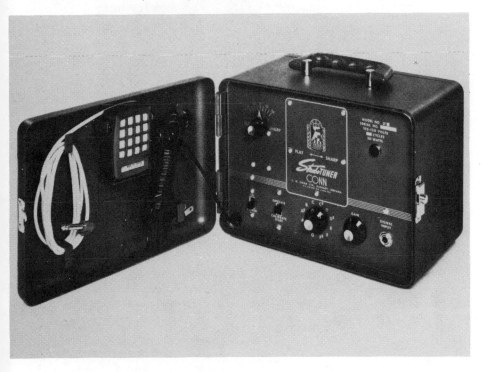

Figure 6–1: THE CONN STROBOTUNER
The Strobotuner visually shows deviation from correct pitch. Photo courtesy of Conn Corporation, Elkhart, Indiana.

Speaking of intonation, I remember being told of a trumpet player who refused to pull his tuning slide because he insisted the instrument was tuned at the factory. The tuning adjustment made at the first intonation lesson, like the one made at the factory, is in no way final. The temperature has a drastic effect on the amount of adjustment necessary. This is why it is so important to warm an instrument before tuning it. As the instrument warms

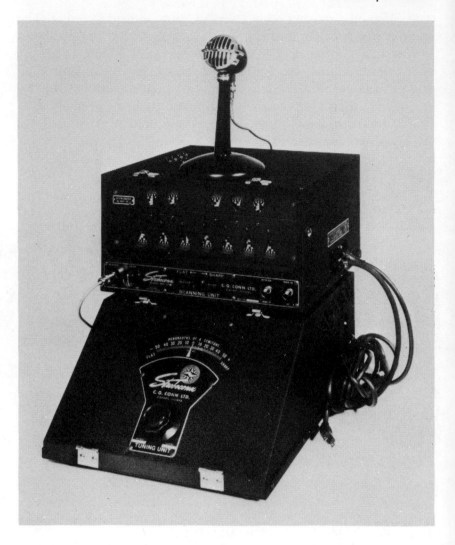

Figure 6–2:   THE STROBOCONN
A player can check any note on his instrument without moving the
dial of this device. Photo courtesy of Conn Corporation, Elkhart,
Indiana.

further under hot stage lights, more adjustment must be made.
Students can be prepared for this by frequent tuning checks
made in rehearsals on the stage under full lights. Even the oboe
will be sharp under these conditions. You may decide to accept
a higher A if the woodwinds can't get down to 440. The impor-

tance of the heat factor must be explained during the intonation lesson.

The strings have a special problem with intonation since a reasonably accurate tempered scale is not built into their instrument as it is in the winds. A muscular memory must be developed in the left hand of string players to enable them to play reliably. This can be developed through trill studies. The procedure is to move between two notes of an interval in half notes until the notes are in tune, then play the interval in quarter notes, eighths, sixteenths, and finally as a trill. The goal is to have the fingers remember the feel of the interval.

Faulty playing position can cause intonation problems. A common example is the girl violinist with long fingernails. The opposite extreme, a violinist playing on the very tips of his fingers, can be equally as bad. This type of mistake that the student has been making for several years is difficult to change, but it must be changed to solve the problem.

You will naturally keep trying to improve the intonation of your players. Ultimately, tuning must rest with each player; his ear must be trained. Given the proper instruction, a school player can be as skilled in intonation as he is in the other aspects of PRITT.

Technique

The constant repetition necessary to acquire a more fluent technique is drudgery to most players, but the teacher must develop methods to have the students do it. Inspiration helps. Show them how fast the chromatic scale can be played after a few months of practice. Lectures on the necessity for gaining technique can be illustrated with examples from the orchestra music that the students are to play. Have them follow their part while a recording is played, or demonstrate by performing it yourself.

Once the students are on their way, see how fast they can play their scales in beats per minute. Use eighth notes for a regular scale and triplets for the chromatic. Challenge each student to learn to play faster. Much as a dieter keeps checking his weight, the players will want to keep checking their technical progress.

Since technique is one area of musicianship where progress is visible, you can keep a record for each student in his personnel folio. The top of the form would read: scale, date assigned, articulation, M.M. 48, 60, 72, etc. Under these headings place the name of the scale, when you assigned it, any special way it is to be played, and the date each metronome mark is passed.

Scale studies are also needed that go throughout the range of the instrument. Fussell's *Ensemble Drill*[2] includes sequential exercises that encompass the entire range of most instruments. Violin notes don't go above fifth position, and lower notes are provided so a player could stay in first position if necessary.

The trill studies that develop the intonation of string players are good for developing the technique of wind players. Tremolo studies in thirds and fourths can be used also. Troublesome combinations should be assigned for practice at home.

TONE

If any one of the five elements of PRITT can be said to be most important, it is tone. A quality of tone must be established that is typical of the instrument. Control of all other elements depends upon a secure tone quality. Without it, intonation cannot be evaluated, rhythm is ineffective, and the phrasing is weak.

Improvement in a student's tone quality is not measurable, but there are things you can do to let him know how he is progressing. A good tape recorder can show a student how his playing sounds to a listener. A professional performer's playing can be put on the same tape for comparison. Use unaccompanied solos for this if available; the recorded sound will be truer, and there will be no distracting elements.

The long tone study is the traditional exercise for developing the tone of a player. Control of the bow (breath for wind players) can be gained by practicing for increased duration of a note. Of course, the volume of the note has a lot to do with how long it can be sustained. Control of pianissimo playing is therefore another benefit that students get from the long tone study. Records of a student's ability to sustain a tone can be kept much as the records of his increasing technical ability. The lower notes require more breath and bow, so if you keep records of a student's progress, make sure to name the exact note used. The form would simply list the note, and you could fill in the duration and the date.

---

[2]Fussell, *Exercises in Ensemble Drill*, pp. 28ff.

Another tone study involves crescendo and diminuendo. Take eight slow beats, four for going from *pp* to *ff* and the other four for *ff* to *pp*. Somewhere around *mf* the sound will probably be much richer than at any other level. The student's task is to enrich his tone at all dynamic levels. String players use a down-bow for the crescendo and an up-bow for the diminuendo. This is opposite to the natural tendency of the bow, but the additional effort required to get the proper effect is good practice. To make the sound louder, the player must: (1) use more pressure on the bow, (2) use a faster bow, (3) approach the bridge with the hair of the bow. Much practice is necessary to find the right proportion of each that will produce the desired effect.

One of the things a teacher can do for string players is demonstrate a solid tone. Bass players especially tend to draw a surface tone from the instrument. It is worth paying a professional bass player to show you how to produce a full sound from the bass.

A full tone can not only be heard on a stringed instrument, it can be seen in the vibration of the thicker strings. A string that is almost still in the middle is sounding the first overtone louder than the fundamental. Part of a string player's tone study time can be profitably spent watching the string. The middle of the vibrating part of the string should always be the area of greatest vibration.

It may be impossible to include all the information and drill presented above about each PRITT skill in one lesson, but once the subject is introduced, it can be followed up in the instructional part of other lessons. After spending a whole period with each subject, the students will know what you mean when you mention any of the PRITT skills.

Orchestra music

The first violin part to a Tchaikovsky overture can't be taught to a high school student in the ten minutes of the lesson that is allotted to studying orchestra music, but you can start him on his way by explaining and drilling one important theme from it. As in all instruction, work with one problem before going to the next. Proceed from notes to rhythm, then work on phrasing, then intonation, perhaps tone, and finally drill progressively toward the proper tempo. Of course, each subject needn't be mastered before discussing the next, but the student must be aware of the improvements he must make in all aspects.

During the work on orchestra music, editorial marks can be added. Phrasing marks are often necessary. Which notes to lengthen, which to shorten, where to breathe or lift the bow, what bowings to use, where to omit or add slurs are all things that can be marked in the students' music. Other marks may be necessary to help players to remember special things you want that aren't in the music. A pair of spectacles sketched above a measure will tell the player that the conductor is going to change tempo at that point and that he should watch carefully. Special cuts or repeats can be marked or checked for accuracy in lessons. Marking the music in lessons also gives you the opportunity to discuss phrasing and the reasons for each editorial mark.

Most of the lesson time devoted to orchestra music must of necessity dwell on problem spots. Sometimes these must be located by playing through a composition, but more often the work on a spot will be planned during an orchestra rehearsal. Keep the plan book handy at rehearsals for this purpose.

Many times the assignment, instruction and drill, and orchestra music parts of the lesson can be combined. You can instruct the students in a part of the orchestra music that will serve as an exercise. Drill on it, and make it the assignment for the following week.

Chamber music

Chamber music makes each member of a group solely responsible for his part. This independence is good for developing self-reliance. Even a conductor is not there to depend on, because the teacher doesn't conduct chamber music; he helps individuals and starts and stops the group.

Later the group can be trained to rehearse itself. A leader is chosen, and he does the starting. Any player stops the group when he suspects something is wrong. Successful groups will want to play through your entire chamber music library; let them—the experience will develop their ability to sight read.

Groups that have little success will have to stick to easier works. Even if you have to transcribe something yourself, provide each class with some kind of chamber music so they can have the experience. A fringe benefit is that a substitute teacher, even one not trained in music, could supervise chamber music rehearsals when you are absent.

Exploit the chamber music for the PRITT training it can give. In a small group players can be aware of the phrasing of the others. The rhythmic training is invaluable; students must think in order to keep their place.

It is possible that a group may do everything well except play in tune. The subtleties of this subject can be taught in a chamber group. The lowest-pitched instrument of the group is used as a reference. Chords are built and sustained on each bass note of a passage, then the rhythmic movement is added in extremely slow motion. As the tempo increases, intonation is still the main subject. If intonation is the one problem, it will improve significantly by this type of drill. If notes (technique) and/or rhythm are problems too, intonation study must be delayed until these two more fundamental elements are under control.

Solos

Developing a player's finesse is a challenging job for a teacher. Progress in this area can be assessed from the student's playing of a solo. Since finesse is to be developed in all students, a solo for each, graded to his technical ability, is required.

The tape recorder is a valuable aid. Using it you can offer comments to the student while his recorded performance is taking place.

Solos can be included in a class lesson. One student plays each week, and the other members of the class can discuss the problems in his solo—the master class procedure.

For especially ambitious players, a solo with orchestral accompaniment can be selected. This should be worked out thoroughly in lessons, preferably a year in advance. A soloist, especially a young one, needs time to learn a piece of music thoroughly. He must be sure nothing will go wrong in the concert. Try many prospective solos with the student to be sure of selecting the one that will show him to best advantage.

Innovative teaching

Some problems in teaching that seem to be insoluble may be worked out by a novel method. Rather than give up on the problems once you've tried all standard methods of dealing with them, give each another try using a new method that you think will work. The experimental approach a student uses to solve his playing problems is also valuable for you in dealing with your teaching problems. Don't deem any of these teaching experiments to be a success or a failure until they've been used on a number of students, however, because the same lesson gets different results from different students.

7 EQUIPPING THE ORCHESTRA

Proper equipment contributes to the success of an orchestra. It speeds progress, inspires teacher and student, and helps to make orchestra the gratifying experience it should be. Of the three requisites the school provides for an orchestra program—equipment, teacher, and physical plant—equipment is the least expensive.

Obtaining equipment

The first step in providing proper equipment for your orchestra is to decide what is needed. Next, prepare a written explanation telling why each item is necessary. Anticipate questions that board members and administrators might ask.

Before presenting your requests, ask colleagues and friends to read your explanations and question you about them. A defense is needed for all items; for instance, if you ask for a harp, be prepared to explain how you are going to find players for it. Delete items that you cannot defend, because one unjustified request casts suspicion on the whole list.

The final step, then, is to prepare your formal proposal and present it through your principal. Include the explanations you have worked out, and introduce the needs by describing the program you wish to provide for the students. Emphasize the fact that all pupils who see the orchestra will benefit educationally if it is fully equipped. Go into detail about the value the program would gain from the added equipment, and mention the disadvantages of continuing without it. Your presentation must persuade the school board to find a way to provide the needed amount of money.

The complete proposal would include: (1) a general introduction explaining the importance of making the orchestra function as much as possible like a professional group, (2) the list of needed equipment, (3) the explanation of the need for each item, (4) prices, and (5) a plan for adding the equipment in several stages. You needn't go into the subject of maintenance costs and expected life of the equipment, but have this information available in case anyone asks for it.

Music

Music is one of the running supplies needed for operating the orchestra. Ask for a music budget as suggested in Chapter 3, and add new numbers to the library each year. Include in your request the necessary music library equipment for storing and keeping track of the music as suggested in Chapter 4.

Chairs

A chair that is correctly shaped helps a player to maintain good playing position. A standard chair is 17 inches high at the back of the seat. The front is normally 18 inches high, but 17½ inches is even more comfortable for playing. Cellists prefer a perfectly horizontal seat that is higher than normal. Short people will be more comfortable on chairs lower than standard. Borrow chairs from other rooms to help you decide which ones to order. Have players of various instruments try them for several rehearsals.

Sturdy construction is taken for granted. Select chairs from a catalog of classroom seating and you will avoid substandard equipment. Select folding chairs only if absolutely necessary. If you are presently using folding chairs, investigate the possibility of replacing them with standard ones.

Stools can be provided for bass players to rest on, even if you want them to stand when they play. For playing, the height is critical, and adjustable stools are the best choice. If used only for resting, thirty-inch stools will suffice.

The tympanist and snare drummer can play from a seated position. All percussionists need a seat to use during the many rests they have. The standard type of drummer's throne is made to be portable. A sturdier adjustable, all-metal stool is available for everyday use; see your classroom seating catalog.

A conductor's stool is a necessity for long rehearsals. For the usual short school rehearsals, it is a matter of preference and personality. If you tend to be impatient with the students, sit—you'll have more patience. If you want your rehearsals to move faster, stand—you'll be less inclined to belabor small details.

Music stands

Every wind and percussion player needs a music stand for his exclusive use. Stands must be available for string players so that there are no more than two persons assigned to each.

Sturdy, all-metal, tubular construction is best. The height and tilt of the ideal student stand can be adjusted with one hand while one foot holds the stand in place. A friction bearing holds the adjustment unless too much weight is on the stand. Because of the weight of the conductor's music, a different type of stand is better for his use, one with a thumb screw to hold the adjustment.

A pencil holder built into a music stand is a desirable feature. Another holder that might be added is one to hold mutes for brass players.

Instruments

Quality is important in a school instrument because of the hard use and careless handling it may get. Fine instruments generally are too delicate for school use, and cheap instruments won't withstand the constant use. The middle-of-the-line instrument will provide years of satisfactory service with little maintenance cost, and it will play better than the regular student model.

It is better to have the parents buy flutes, clarinets, trumpets, and violins. The investment will prompt them to see that the instrument is used regularly; the student will practice more and be less likely to drop out of orchestra.

To start an orchestra in the high school, oboes, bassoons, French horns, basic percussion equipment, a piano, violas, cellos, and basses must be provided. Besides the number needed for orchestra, training instruments may be required to prepare oboe, bassoon, horn, viola, cello, and bass players to take the place of people who will be graduating. Players can be changed from other instruments to these if the instruments are available. Of course, if you are sure a sufficient supply of trained players will enter your school each year, no training instruments are necessary.

Adding a bass clarinet, English horn, tuba, more percussion equipment, and some violins will improve the orchestra. When the program is established, add a bass trombone, some A clarinets, saxophones, more percussion equipment, and some better-quality stringed instruments. To make the orchestra have full symphonic capabilities, add the alto flute, contrabassoon, D trumpets, complete percussion equipment, and some fine quality stringed instruments. Also add a harpsichord to make possible an authentic rendition of baroque literature. Add a harp if you can train players for it.

If the quality of flutes, clarinets, trumpets, trombones, and violins provided by the students is inadequate, the players should be encouraged to buy new ones with greater capabilities. The school should have some of these on hand to loan to students in hardship cases.

Maintenance and replacement

Instruments will receive good care if the students are instructed in maintenance procedures. Even so, repairs will be necessary periodically because of the normal wear on the moving parts of the instrument.

Bows will have to be rehaired once or twice a year, depending upon the amount of use they get. Bow hair is often broken by a clumsy stroke, making the need for new hair obvious. Even though it looks good, it needs to be replaced if it won't hold rosin any longer.

Strings are likely to break after a year of hard use. They must be replaced if the winding comes loose. Better strings last longer. Chrome steel strings are more durable than wound strings.

Woodwind instruments have the most moving parts. Though the distance travelled is slight, the frequency of operation causes wear.

Brass and percussion instruments are the easiest to maintain. Sometimes the tone of a brass instrument can be restored just by a good cleaning. For some items of percussion instrument maintenance, see Chapter 10.

As an automobile becomes unreliable after a great number of miles, so does an instrument that has played a great number of notes. If major repairs are performed on a certain instrument two or more times, a replacement is needed. This generally comes between seven and ten years for wind instruments. One advantage of the orchestra is that good stringed instruments seldom need to be replaced. They will outlast several cases.

The date of purchase for a particular instrument in your inventory will give you a general indication of when it should be replaced; however, if the instrument has lain unused for some years, it will last much longer than one that has been in the hands of one ambitious student after another. Because of this, a strict rotating replacement plan is a questionable policy. A better plan would be to use the allotted money to replace the instruments that are in the worst condition.

Selection of instruments

A satisfactory experience with a certain make of instrument will encourage you to select it again. An unsatisfactory experience with a certain model will naturally prompt you to look for one that is more suitable. Other teachers can let you know how the model they use stands up under school care. Friends who specialize on the instrument in question will be happy to advise you. Music dealers know much about the quality of an instrument from the repairs they're called on to make. Catalogs help if they give specifications that you're interested in.

Features to look for on woodwinds are: soft, flexible pads that will seat completely over the tone holes; well-anchored posts that will hold the necessary alignment; thorough bracing of all long rods; screw adjustments on many keys; keys of hard metal, not easily bent.

Double horns with the conventional string linkage are best for orchestra. Trumpets should be equipped with a first or third valve trigger to enable one or both of these valve slides to be extended when necessary. The tuba should have a fourth valve to make better intonation possible on certain notes. Large bore brass instruments should be avoided for young players.

Criteria for selection of percussion instruments will be listed in Chapter 10.

The catalog description of various models of stringed instru-

ments are almost the same. All acceptable instruments have gen-
uine ebony fittings, an acceptable bow, a sturdy plush-lined case,
and shop adjustments already made. Better instruments are made
of carefully selected, seasoned woods, and they are furnished
with a pernambuco bow. They will be made better, because a
maker will take more time on an instrument that is made of better
materials.

The adjustment of a stringed instrument is a critical factor. The
nut across which the strings ride must be the right height so that
the first finger can play notes next to it with minimum effort. The
bridge must be low enough that a finger pressing one string
doesn't get stuck under the neighboring string. If the bridge is too
low, the strings will buzz against the fingerboard during playing.

Plywood cellos and basses have a sound that is inferior to natural wood instruments. They may be a logical choice, however,
because of their endurance and resistance to cracking. Student
cellists should be encouraged to buy natural wood instruments.
Some of each can be supplied by the school, the better players
using the better instruments.

When purchasing an instrument for the school, you will be
asked to describe it on a requisition form. List all specifications
that you feel are important, including unacceptable features.
State the make and model of instrument if you know one that is
exactly what you want; otherwise, have the dealers submit bids
on several makes and models from which you can choose.

Accessories

Another part of the budget for running supplies will be used
for accessories. Supplies for keeping the instruments operating
properly should be on hand. Other accessories are necessary for
the orchestra to function, some of them expendable supplies and
some permanent items.

Accessories needed for woodwinds are: cork grease, swabs,
cleaning rods, large feathers for removing moisture, reeds, and
fingering charts. Oboists need tuning forks and reed tools. Used
only occasionally are bore oil and key oil.

Brass instrument accessories include: grease for valve slides
and tuning slides, valve oil, slide oil, and fingering charts. For
cleaning, a wire snake is helpful. Pipe cleaners and small brushes

are needed for cleaning mouthpieces of brass and reed instruments.

Horn players use only one type of mute regularly, a nontransposing one. Trumpet and trombone players need straight and cup mutes made of heavy fiber. The metal mute with an adjustable plunger is known as a Harmon mute. It is often usable in place of a cup mute to provide a more penetrating sound. For the best effect, all mutes should be identical in construction, so it is best if the school provides them. Good mutes will last several years.

Accessories needed for stringed instruments are: rosin, a fournote pitch pipe, and a mute. Most violinists and violists need a shoulder rest. Bass rosin must be supplied in several degrees of hardness.

Cleaning preparations made for stringed instruments dissolve rosin that is caked on the strings and instrument without damaging either in any way. A polish made for stringed instruments can be applied after the cleaning preparation has been used. To be sure students use the correct cleaner and polish, have the school furnish it.

The question of whether to provide the orchestra with uniforms has often been raised, the theory being that the attraction of the band uniform lures students away from orchestra. You will have to decide this in the light of your situation. Judging from photos in periodicals and appearances of orchestras at conferences, most directors do not think uniforms are necessary.

Music stand lights are necessary if the orchestra is to function in the pit. Choose lights that extend high enough above the stand to permit easy turning of pages. The angle of the panel should be adjustable so the player can keep it from shining into the audience.

The conductor needs a podium. Elaborate models include a light and storage space. The podium must be constructed solidly so that it won't squeak when you shift your weight on it.

A cabinet used to store running supplies should have many shallow shelves so that you can locate materials quickly. In addition to the accessories listed previously, you will want to have emergency repair supplies on hand: pads, penetrating oil, a mouthpiece puller, a soundpost setter, small screw drivers, corks, peg composition, etc. An emergency repair kit will provide you with the items that you need. In addition to some of the above items it will include a mallet, a knife, a spring hook, and other small tools and supplies.

Teaching aids

Orchestral performance demands synchronized action that is only possible with perfect understanding. Diverse aids help to impart this understanding faster and with less drill.

It will be easy to make some teaching aids if you keep the necessary materials on hand. Visual aids can be made using illustration board and a felt-tipped marker. Flash card stock consisting of a blank staff is available and convenient to use. Audio aids that you will want to make necessitate having tape recording accessories and blank tape on hand. The shop teacher, art teacher, and the audio-visual aids specialist are too busy to make aids for you, but they will be glad to teach you how to make them.

A record player and tape recorder are almost indispensable in teaching orchestra. An amplifier or pre-amplifier added makes it possible to put sections of records on tape. Extension speakers are needed if the player and tape recorder are not part of a console. Headphones are ideal for individual listening.

Two items that will get so much use they will seldom be in the cabinet are the electronic tuner and the metronome. These and the chalkboard and bulletin board are the aids that will be used daily.

Other aids are available within the school. These are: 16mm. movie projector, film strip projector, slide projector, opaque projector, overhead projector, portable public address system, central sound system, and the auditorium sound system. Perhaps your school has a 16mm. movie camera, a video tape recorder and camera, and more.

Books are great aids to learning in other subjects, and they can help in orchestra also. Musical scores, complete with recordings, can circulate from the music library or the main library. History and appreciation books can be provided that are more advanced than those that would be of interest to the general school population. Periodicals dealing with music should be received in the music department and placed within easy access of students.

The reference library of the music department should include dictionaries of music and musicians, instrumental technique reference books, instrument repair manuals, music catalogs, foreign language dictionaries, music and music education books and periodicals, conducting manuals, and reference scores.

Office equipment

The director's office should adjoin the rehearsal room. In a typical design, the door would be in the center of one wall of the office with large windows on both sides taking up the rest of that wall.

As you enter the office, a sink is on your left. It has a light above and storage space below. The sink has a mixing faucet with a rinser hose attachment. A large drainboard is provided. Along the same wall is a small desk with a copying machine on it. Open shelves are above and below the desk. A long work table, desk high and open underneath, takes up the rest of that wall. Shelves are mounted on the wall above the work table. Electric outlets are provided, as they are on all walls.

Against the wall opposite the door is an accessory cabinet and some open shelves to accommodate a tape recorder, microphones, and reference books. Against the wall to your right is a sorting rack.

Beside the door, facing the window, is the office desk. The master control station of an intercom system is on it. On the wall beside the desk is a small bulletin board.

The office just described is functional. If it is soundproofed, lessons can be given in it also. The only unusual feature, the intercom, is available at a cost less than that of a student model flute. Many homes are equipped with them. One that permits calls to be initiated from any of the remote stations should be selected.

Rehearsal room equipment

Sound conditioning is necessary to limit the amount of reverberation in the rehearsal room. Aids are: a high, irregularly shaped ceiling; non-parallel, sound-treated walls; and a small window area. An existing room can be improved by draping large window areas and adding panels of acoustical tile or styrofoam blocks to break up large wall areas.

The lighting in the rehearsal room should be more intense than in a regular classroom because the players are reading at a greater then normal distance. Skylights built into the room provide light that is free of glare.

Before giving specifications for a new room or deciding upon renovations to an old one, visit other communities to see what has been done. Ask directors about the features of their rooms. If an architect is involved in your project, make sure he knows what purposes the room must serve and what features you expect to be incorporated in it.

Collapsible risers belong on stage where they will be used only intermittently. The permanent risers built into the rehearsal room should extend from wall to wall. For safety, the lip of each riser should be a contrasting color.

Many new buildings have wall-to-wall carpeting instead of tile on the floor. This is particularly good in the rehearsal room for the acoustical effect. Watch for loose edges.

The rehearsal room should be larger than the performing area of your stage, not only for acoustical reasons, but also to enable persons seated on the outside of the orchestra to see the chalkboard. Also, if the room is shallow, the conductor is forced so close to the players that he cannot judge the balance.

A projection screen can be installed above the chalkboard at the front of the rehearsal room. Darkening curtains necessary for effective projection can serve also as acoustical treatment for the windows.

Also at the front of the room should be a phonograph-tape recorder console. Storage space for records and tapes is needed nearby in a locked cabinet. Keep the console away from the chalkboard; chalk dust ruins records and tape recorders.

Another area that is used for both rehearsal and performance is the orchestra pit. In most schools it is not adequate for an orchestra. Removing a row or two of auditorium seats will enlarge the pit area if it is on floor level. A balustrade makes the area look like an orchestra pit, and a heavy cloth can be hung from it to further isolate the orchestra from the audience. Excess orchestral volume can be decreased by hanging a heavy cloth in front of the stage and installing carpeting on the floor of the pit.

A new school should be provided with a sunken pit. Receptacles installed in the floor of the pit enable players to plug in stand lights without the need for wires lying on the floor. Perhaps a foot pedal rheostat control could be put into the circuit at the conductor's place so that he could not only switch the lights on and off noiselessly, but also regulate the intensity of them.

Practice room equipment

Acoustical tile on the walls and carpeting on the floor are required to make the sound of an instrument tolerable in a small room. Non-treated rooms with large windows can be used for study areas. One of these can be fitted as a library where students can study scores, listen to recordings, write music, or study theory. All rooms should be in the direct view of the conductor.

At least one practice room should have a full-length mirror to enable students to study their playing form. A small shelf in each room would be convenient.

The intercom system should have a remote station in each practice room. Also, an outlet is needed to make possible the use of electronic teaching aids. A master switch governing practice room current will make it possible for you to turn off all lights without having to enter each practice room.

Storage facilities

Instrument and music storage is convenient in rooms adjoining the rehearsal room. Entrance and exit doors to the instrument room permit a smooth traffic flow. Music should be stored in the room next to the director's office. If possible, it should also have two doors—one to the rehearsal room and one to the office.

The music library is a normal room with regular classroom lighting. It is furnished with cabinets and/or shelves, a large table, a sorting rack, a small bulletin board, and an intercom remote station.

The instrument room is a normal room, but it must be large enough to accommodate the orchestra members, since almost all of them will be in it at once. Instrument storage compartments must be built into the room. Each one should be able to hold a music folio in addition to the instrument for which it is designed. Lockers should be provided to guard expensive small instruments against theft.

Cabinets with locks should be available for storing things in the most convenient place—record storage near the phonograph, accessories near the instruments, repair supplies near the work bench, etc. Cabinets could be used in the rehearsal room, the instrument room, the office, and the music library.

Auditorium equipment

The school auditorium is the setting for performances. The players will want to be heard to best advantage there, and some special equipment is needed to make this possible.

Stages are designed for plays, and the lights are aimed at the actors. This type of lighting is distracting to people trying to read music. For concerts, the lights shining toward the eyes of the players must be dimmed. The red and blue stage lights can also be dimmed to provide a better light for reading. Some color is necessary to make the complexion of the players look natural.

Another reason for dimming lights is to reduce excess heat on the stage. Turn stage lights off during intermissions. The best solution to the heat problem is a quiet air-conditioning system. The next best is a set of exhaust fans at the top of the flies and the top of the auditorium. The fans will make too much noise at high speed, but they can be turned on low speed during a performance.

Risers are necessary to let the audience see all players. The risers on the stage should be similar to the ones built into the rehearsal room to preserve balance as it is worked out in rehearsals.

Select safe risers. Collapsible legs are dangerous because student assistants often fail to lock the legs in the upright position. A rough surface on the risers helps prevent chairs from slipping. Appearance is a minor consideration since the risers will be hidden by the players anyway. Risers that lock together eliminate the possibility of a chair leg slipping between them.

An acoustical shell projects the sound of the orchestra toward the audience. If it is straight across the stage, the sound will not be focused toward a particular section of the auditorium. Panels placed above the orchestra as a sort of roof prevent a large part of the sound from escaping into the flies. Ropes holding these panels can be used to draw them up (fly them) when not in use.

Much special equipment is needed in the auditorium for producing musicals. This is missing in older schools, but new ones should provide it. A special sound system, a sunken orchestra pit, an intercom system, complete lighting provisions for the pit and the stage, a large backstage area, and dressing rooms are easier to put into a new school than they are to add to an existing one.

Chamber music needs a more intimate setting than a large audi-torium. A small lecture hall is better if one is available. If not, the rehearsal room will serve. The audience occupies the orchestra seats, and the players sit where the podium usually is. A few special lights shine on the performers, and a temporary shell—perhaps one made from stage scenery flats—stands behind them.

The smaller audience attracted by chamber music will seem larger in a small room, and the character of the music will be preserved. A new building might incorporate a small stage at the front of the rehearsal room.

8 IMPROVING THE STRING SECTION

A balanced string section with all members using the bow neatly and playing the notes at the right time, in tune, with vibrato, is an ideal not easily achieved. Work toward this end involves procuring the necessary instruments, as stated in Chapter 7, and providing careful instruction. Many deficiencies in school string sections are due to a lack of understanding and skill in basic bowing and fingering. These subjects must be constantly reviewed. Repeated drill on new skills is also necessary to make sure that the players have them at their command when they are needed.

Balancing the section

There are two aspects of balance, one on paper and one in sound. A numerical balance may sound unbalanced because of weak players or poor instruments within any one section. Attaining a balance of comparable players in each section is the important objective. It may be necessary to appeal to certain players to switch instruments. This is best approached on an individual basis; decide which players would do a good job on the instrument needed, and talk to them in private. You might be doing them a favor. Playing opportunities are greater for players of the lower strings than they are for violinists. Likely candidates for viola are violinists who don't like to play high notes. Violinists with poor playing position may turn out to be outstanding cellists. A boy with very thick, strong fingers could use his violin training to enable him to become a fluent bassist quickly. An unsuccessful practice is to switch players with little ability. They are no asset to their new section, and the sound remains unbalanced. Switching outstanding players is undesirable because it leaves the section from which they came weaker.

The numerical balance is not a life-or-death factor in the orchestral sound. If all players are comparable in all sections, a 10-10-4-6-3 string section will not sound so very different from the more ideal 10-8-6-4-2. In fact, the switching of two second violinists to viola would result in a quite acceptable section, 10-8-6-6-3.

Weak players in a section present a problem. They can be helped by a good leader and additional players. Adding too many weak players could become a process of the blind leading the blind, but a few extra players in the section are a help. A 10-12-6-4-2 section might sound more balanced than it appears.

The seating within each section can be arranged to help the weaker players. Seat a good player beside a weak player. This puts the better players on the outside of the orchestra. A richer sound as well as a better appearance should be instantaneous. Thus, in a section of ten violins, the sixth in ability will sit beside the first-chair player, the seventh beside the second, eighth beside the third, ninth beside the fourth, and the tenth beside the fifth.

On a school stage the outside strings of the orchestra are usually in front of the curtain line. Seating a weak section in this position can help the balance. To be sure, the first violins must always be at the conductor's left, but various major symphonies use different seating plans for the other sections. Some place the cellos to the conductor's right, others the violas, and others the second violins. If the bass section is not large, the first desk of basses can be on the edge of the stage.

Weak instruments are a handicap in a string section. The installation of chrome steel strings will bring about a stronger sound, even though the tone may not be more pleasing. Basses especially profit from the steel strings. Make sure the repairman lowers the bridge somewhat when installing these strings; they are harder to push down than the regular strings. On instruments other than basses, an adjuster must be mounted on the tailpiece for each steel string. These strings are too sensitive to tune using the tuning peg.

The only thing you can do to insure a balance of good-sounding instruments is to have the school provide some of each type that you can assign to the stronger players. Until this is possible, you can appeal to students who are able to buy better instruments to do so.

In short, to bring about a balanced sound in the string section, you can (1) switch some players to other instruments, (2) assign good leaders to all sections, (3) assign some extra players to a weak section, (4) seat strong players beside weaker players, (5) provide weak instruments with steel strings, (6) purchase some good instruments of all types for school ownership, (7) arrange the seating to favor weaker sections.

Tuning the instrument

A primary cause of out-of-tune playing is out-of-tune strings. Turning the tuning peg and pushing it in at the same time with one hand is physically difficult. Most players are not ready to do this before their freshman year in high school. At that time it should be taught, because it is necessary to bow the instrument while it is being tuned. The procedure of holding the instrument with one hand and turning the peg with the other will have to suffice until the student is able to do it the better way.

When the player can manipulate the peg with one hand, he can tune each string in relation to the one previously tuned. Playing on two open strings at once, he turns the peg of the string being tuned until the hollow sound of the perfect fifth is obtained.

Out-of-tune open strings in the orchestra probably are the result of mistuned A strings. The student is too easily satisfied. If his A is close to the pitch of the oboe, he doesn't consider it worth retuning. It really isn't all his fault.

First of all, the oboe player has to be prepared to sustain a correct A long enough and loud enough for the full string section to hear. Since this is unduly taxing on the oboist, an electronic A is preferable. The matching of this A must be perfect. It can be checked by sounding the harmonic produced by placing a finger lightly in the middle of the string. The resulting octave-higher pitch is easier to hear, especially if the wind instruments are tuning at the same time.

Basses tune using the harmonics in third position, the first finger harmonic on the thicker string matching the fourth finger harmonic on the neighboring higher string. (See Figure 8–1.) The other instruments can tune using the harmonics in fourth position. (See Figure 8–2.) A final check of the accuracy of the tuning is to play these harmonics as a double stop. Playing on both strings at once with the fingers producing the correct harmonic on each should produce a perfect unison.

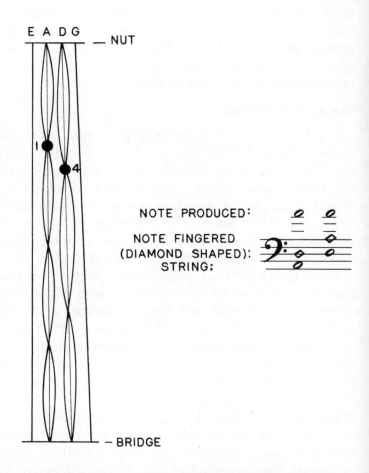

Figure 8–1: TUNING THE BASS BY MEANS OF HARMONICS
The fingers touch the strings lightly as shown. The D string vibrating in thirds produces the same note as the A string vibrating in fourths.

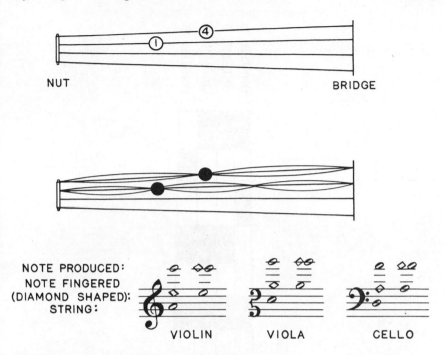

NOTE PRODUCED:
NOTE FINGERED
(DIAMOND SHAPED):
STRING:

VIOLIN   VIOLA   CELLO

Figure 8–2:   TUNING USING HARMONICS
The fingers in fourth position touch the strings lightly as shown. The thinner string vibrating in halves produces the same note as the one beside it vibrating in thirds.

Reviewing fundamental left hand technique

The refinement of intonation is not possible if the student lacks the concept of the fingerboard as a keyboard where every different note requires a different placement of the finger. The keyboard concept is so simple for a pianist to acquire, yet so difficult for a string player. The piano keyboard has white keys for naturals and black keys for sharps and flats; the string player often doesn't know where to find a sharp or flat.

To get a view of this problem, look at the fingerboard of the violin if the "white and black keys" were to be painted on it. (Figure 8–3.) The difficulty is that most, but not all, of the naturals are beside each other across the fingerboard. Is it any wonder the student plays F-sharp on the E string when he wants F natural? Violin teachers from Leopold Mozart on have complained about that note.

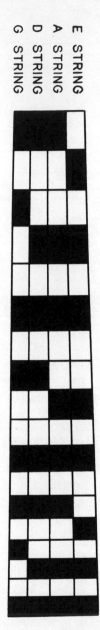

Figure 8–3: THE VIOLIN "KEYBOARD"
The fingerboard of the violin would look this way if the keys were to be painted on it to correspond to the white and black keys of the piano.

The first step in improving string intonation is to make sure each student has this keyboard concept of the fingerboard and that he knows where to find every sharp and flat. The next step is to teach him that though the "keyboard" looks that way, it doesn't feel that way. For instance, the finger placement for the A-flat scale on the violin looks like Figure 8–4, but it feels like Figure 8–5. The fingers feel close together for half steps and far

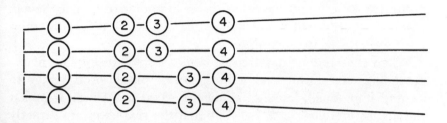

Figure 8–4: THE VIOLIN A-FLAT SCALE (APPEARANCE)
Measuring half and whole-step distances would produce this pattern for the fingers to strike in playing the A-flat scale.

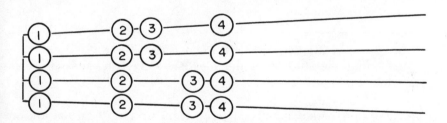

Figure 8–5: THE VIOLIN A-FLAT SCALE (FEEL)
Judging by the pitches produced, the pattern of finger placement for the A-flat scale feels this way.

apart for whole steps. The disconcerting fact is that a whole step feels bigger than two half steps. When the student is aware of these things, he is on the road to improving his intonation.

The third step is to drill the student on his intervals. Each violinist and violist must learn how far apart the fingers are for half steps, whole steps, augmented seconds, minor thirds (the fingering of these two intervals is different, though they sound the same), major thirds, perfect fourths, and augmented fourths (diminished fifths). From there on it is easy because the perfect fifth is straight across the string from the starting note, the minor sixth feels like a half step except the fingers are on different strings, the major sixth feels like a whole step, the minor seventh like a minor third, the major seventh like a major third, and the octave like a perfect fourth. A similar type of training is appropriate for cellists and bassists. The trill studies of Otakar Sevcik (Opus 7, several editions available) can be adapted for this training, as suggested in Chapter 6.

When the student has trouble remembering the finger placement for a certain interval, a mark can be placed on the page to remind him. The ⋀ sign connecting two notes indicates that the fingers are close, ⌐⌐ means that the two notes are directly across the string from each other, as shown in Figure 8–6.

Figure 8–6:   MARKING FINGER PLACEMENT
Reminding the student of the location of certain notes prevents some intonation problems.

Marking finger placement can often clear up faulty intonation on higher notes, as in Figure 8–7.

Figure 8–7:   HIGH NOTE FINGER PLACEMENT
High passages that present potential intonation problems can be marked before the music is distributed.

With the finger trying for the correct distance and the instrument accurately tuned, the pitch will be close to correct. From here it must be refined by the player until it sounds right. When the finger is close to the correct pitch, a slight change in the angle of the finger on the string will be enough to bring the note into focus. Without the knowledge discussed above, the student stands little chance of coming this close to correct pitch.

Training the player to refine the pitch and bring it into focus is a process of having him match pitches as when he was learning the intervals. This can be developed with the full orchestra. Take a chord apart and put it back together from the basses up. Have each note sustained until the section agrees upon the pitch. If this doesn't work, you will probably find that the open strings are out of tune. Unison scales in sustained notes provide drill in this type of pitch matching.

To recapitulate, each player should learn to tune his instrument with one hand so the other is free to bow. Bowing two strings at once, the student can tune in perfect fifths. Basses tune by the natural harmonics, and the tuning of the other stringed instruments can be checked by using them also. The student will come close to the note if he understands the fingerboard as a keyboard, is drilled on the intervals, and is reminded by marks in the music of finger placement that he tends to forget. Refinement of the pitches can be stressed in group playing, where matching pitches is necessary.

Teaching the fingerboard

The entire fingerboard can be explained by the keyboard analogy previously mentioned, with emphasis on the shrinking physical size of the intervals approaching the bridge as illustrated in Figure 8–3.

Exercises must be assigned to put this concept to use. Sequential exercises such as the one in Figure 8–8 are helpful in teaching the feel of the higher positions. The hand must contract gradually as each higher position is used.

The shifting procedure itself must be studied and accuracy developed. All fingers deserve a chance, but the first and second are by far the most commonly used shifting fingers. Figure 8–9 shows a scale-line shifting exercise where the finger moves one scale de-

gree at a time. Figure 8–10 shows the shifting motion that is used
more often where the finger moves two scale degrees at a time.

Figure 8–8: VIOLIN SEQUENTIAL EXERCISE
Drills such as this provide an introduction to the upper areas of the
fingerboard. Similar drills can be written for the other stringed instruments.

Figure 8–9: VIOLA SHIFTING DRILL
This exercise dwells on the type of position change that would be
necessary in an exercise such as Figure 8–8. Isolating the shift for drill
this way eliminates other problems, enabling the student to concentrate on shifting.

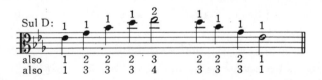

Figure 8–10: TYPICAL SHIFTING DRILL
A shift that raises each finger two notes higher than it was is more
useful than a shift moving only one note. Here just the shifting is practiced. As in all exercises, the descent should be practiced. Descending
shifting is harder; it should be practiced even more than the ascent.

On the violin and viola, the thumb knuckle must support the instrument as usual, except at the moment of shifting. At that instant the shoulder and chin grip the instrument so it will not move. Once the shift is completed, the normal grip is resumed. The finger also releases its pressure on the string during a shift; if a student rubs the skin from his fingertips practicing shifting, you have neglected to tell him this important principle. The bow also must relax its pressure during a shift to help cover the sound of the moving finger.

Practicing double stops is a way of learning the correct relationship between the fingers as the shifts take place. Even if the intervals are played slightly out of tune, the student learns the basic position of the fingers progressing up the fingerboard. To get the full benefit, he should shift all fingers, not one at a time. In other words, the fingers must always lie above their notes, curved, never collapsed. The octave exercise makes the correct position imperative on the violin and viola. (See Figure 8–11.)

Figure 8–11: OCTAVE DOUBLE STOPS
Students will not play this exercise in tune, but it helps to bring about the correct relation of the first and fourth fingers in the different positions.

The thumb moves with the fingers, always in a position to accept the weight of the instrument. (See Figure 8–12.)

The same type of exercise can be played on the cello using the first and third fingers as shown in Figure 8–13.

Figure 8–14 shows the exercise written for bass. The first and fourth fingers produce the interval of a perfect fifth. Above G, the third finger is used instead of the fourth.

All of these exercises can be played by rote, and indeed, the students will not learn to read the high notes just by playing

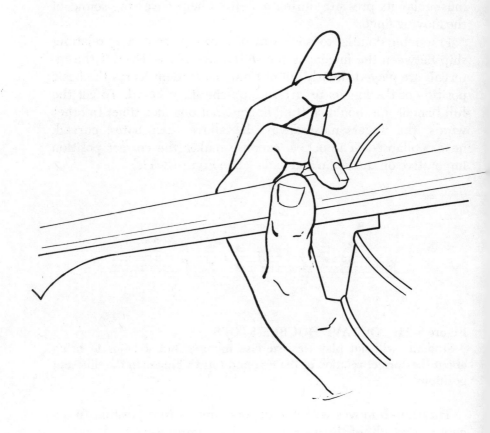

Figure 8–12: THUMB LOCATION
   The lower picture shows typical mistakes made by a player just learning to play the high notes on the violin or viola. The upper pic-

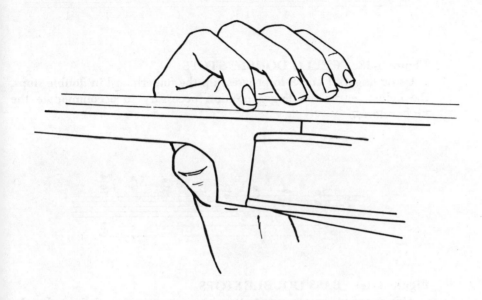

ture shows the thumb correctly under the neck and all fingers over the notes to be played.

Figure 8–13:   CELLO DOUBLE STOPS
Using fingers 1 and 3 to progress up the fingerboard in double stops, the cellist learns the finger position necessary to accommodate the higher notes.

Figure 8–14:   BASS DOUBLE STOPS
This exercise corresponds to the octave exercise for violin and viola. On the bass, the notes above G in the middle of the G string are played with the third finger instead of the fourth.

them. One way to teach the student to read high notes is to have them play songs they know, but written an octave higher. Familiar songs using high notes will also help to teach this area of the fingerboard because the students can effectively match pitches with their mental image of the notes. (See Figure 8–15.)

Figure 8–15:   FAMILIAR SONG
Capitalize on the student's familiarity with a song to teach him something using it. High notes can be taught this way.

The student just learning the high notes will want to shift back to first position at every opportunity. This is not bad—first position playing is more brilliant—but it is often cumbersome. He needs to know how to play in the higher position on all strings. This can be explained to him simply by pointing out that the relationship of notes across the string in higher positions is the same as first position. For example, if the student is playing the note F on his first string, he can figure what lies across the string from the note F down an octave, in first position. The same note lies across from it in the higher octave. By the same reasoning, since F and A are not straight across the string from each other in first position, they are not straight across in the higher position. (Figure 8–16 illustrates the foregoing.) After this explanation, the student is ready to practice études in the higher positions.

The complete fingerboard can be taught effectively by (1) using the keyboard analogy with the "keys" becoming progressively smaller toward the bridge, (2) using sequential exercises to progress up the "keys," (3) drilling on the shifting procedure, (4) using double stops to teach correct hand and finger position, (5) teaching the high notes using familiar songs, (6) explaining high note relationships in terms of octave-lower, first position relationships, and (7) assigning études in the higher positions.

Figure 8–16: RELATIONSHIPS ACROSS THE STRING
Since B-flat is straight across from F in first position, it is also straight across in a higher position. Since F and A are played with fingers close in first position, they are also close in a higher position.

The changing clef for viola and cello

The treble clef often used in viola music and the tenor clef of cello music cause problems in the school orchestra. The passages using them are usually the most difficult in the piece being played.

Teaching the new clefs is almost like asking the students to learn a new language. A complicating factor is that these clefs utilize the higher notes—notes with which the students are less familiar.

An orchestral passage using the clef will provide motivation for the students to learn to read it. Mark the fingering and the half steps in one such passage. In drilling the players on the passage, make a trill study out of each interval; this will give them a chance to associate the notes on the page with what they're playing.

The traditional introduction to a new clef uses scales running from the old clef into the new. Start work on these by having the student say the name of each note as he plays it. It is important for him to know the name of the note in order that he may judge the finger placement and find the right pitch. Test his learning with flash cards. Treble clef flash cards are available, and you can make some for tenor clef using flash card stock. Have him name and play the note on each card.

Another introduction to the new clef you can provide is a few landmarks to help the student get oriented. If he remembers where the open A string and the harmonic A in the middle of the string are notated, he can figure out the location of other notes. He can also easily remember the note on the top line of the staff; it is the first note beyond first position on the A string.

Written assignments help the student to learn a new clef. Ask him to use it to rewrite excerpts from an orchestra part. He will better understand the need for the different clef when he sees how many ledger lines are eliminated.

The first étude a student plays in the new clef should be one with which he is familiar. Transcribe one that he knows, or even better, have him transcribe it. The second might be a familiar song written in the new clef and using high notes. After a thorough introduction and these preliminary études, the student is ready to study études in the new clef. It is also important that he practice music that changes back and forth between the clefs. This mental "shifting gears" requires practice.

Certain similarities exist between the fingering of the clefs. Notes on the lines of the viola staff and the treble use fingers 1 or 3 in the odd-numbered positions; playing a tenor clef note on the cello is possible by thinking in bass clef but playing one string higher. You can point out these similarities to get a student started quickly in the new clef, but key signatures and accidentals will influence the new clef in a way that he will not grasp without the systematic study described in the preceding paragraphs.

Vibrato

The development of this aspect of playing aids the tone of the player greatly. The old idea was to delay this teaching until the student played perfectly in tune. A student who plays long enough to develop his intonation to a high degree also develops a habit of not vibrating that becomes difficult to break. He is used to being still on the note; to get him to move continually is like teaching him to play all over again. The student will ask how vibrato is done at some point in his playing career, and this is your chance to get him working on it. If his bowing is secure, he has a chance of success.

Three fundamental principles give the greatest degree of freedom to the development of a vibrato. (1) The base knuckle of the finger must leave the neck of the instrument, the knuckle of the thumb rolling under the neck to support it (this principle doesn't apply to the cello and bass). (2) Only one finger is used on the fingerboard at a time, the vibrato passing from one finger to another. (3) The finger rolls between its regular height and a lower height. (See Figures 8–17 and 8–18.) The third principle, the finger rolling between regular and low position, requires some explanation because we know that the pitch we hear is in the center of the vibrato. The finger position doesn't go above normal, however, because of the clumsiness of this high position. (See Figure 8–19.) In other words, the regular position of the finger (Figure 8–18) when using vibrato produces a pitch that would be somewhat sharp if it were sustained.

Freedom in experimenting with the vibrato on the violin and viola is gained by a sure support of the instrument. Have the player put the scroll of the instrument against the wall. (Use a sponge between to avoid scratching the instrument.) This way the student will be able to let the base knuckle of the fingers leave the neck with no fear that the instrument will fall. Guide the student's experimentation by placing your thumb and a finger on the knuckles of the finger he's trying to make vibrate. Move the finger back and forth between the regular and low position. As you do

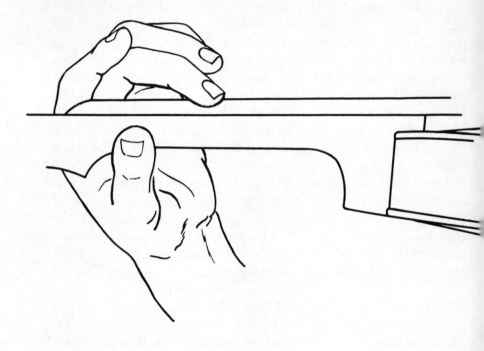

Figure 8–17: LOW POSITION
  The vibrating finger rolls to a position lower than normal as part of every vibration.

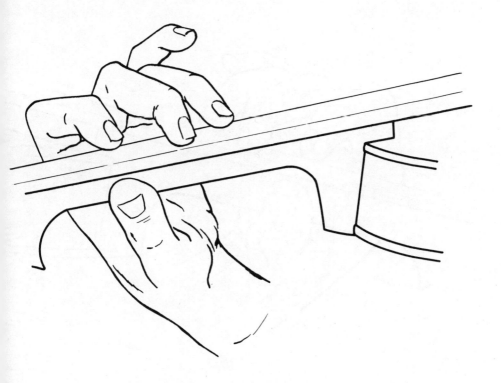

Figure 8–18:   REGULAR POSITION
   The regular position of a finger on the string has the finger rounded
and inclined toward the player.

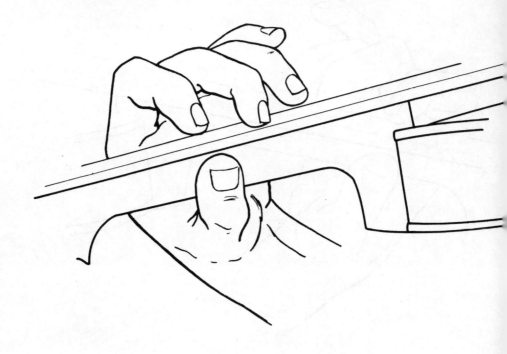

Figure 8–19: HIGH POSITION
The position with the first joint of the finger perpendicular to the fingerboard is clumsy, even as part of a vibrato. This position is *not* used.

this, the student can judge how much cooperation of the arm and wrist is necessary.

Once the student learns the motion, he must develop it. This can be done by vibrating in rhythm, getting progressively faster. Some students will immediately develop the motion by following the teacher's example. The habit of vibrating must then be developed. The lesson on vibrato will soon be forgotten unless the teacher continually insists upon the use of vibrato whenever applicable.

The speed of the vibrato changes with the expression of the music and the register of the note being played. In general, the higher the note, the faster the vibrato. The cello vibrato is slower than the violin vibrato, for example, and also the vibrato on the viola C string is not as fast as on the A string of the same instrument.

The width of the vibrato, how far the finger moves, depends largely on the expression in the music. The intense romanticism of Tchaikovsky calls for a faster, wider vibrato than the restrained classicism of Haydn.

Students may be reluctant to use a vibrato they know to be too slow or too narrow, but in a string section these individual weaknesses don't stand out. Even a poor vibrato helps a player because of the additional bow pressure he will use when trying to vibrate.

The teaching of vibrato has been a subject of many articles in music-teaching periodicals. The main ideas presented here are the three principles that help the student develop it, namely: (1) the finger knuckle doesn't touch the neck, (2) one finger at a time is on the fingerboard, (3) the finger rolls between the regular position and a lower position.

Nuances of the vibrato aid the musical expression. The detached slur (*parlando, portato,* or *louré*) is aided by a stopping of the vibrato to accompany the stopping of the bow. A speeding up of the vibrato aids the effect of a crescendo. Soft notes need a fast, narrow vibrato. The work of soloists should be studied to discover how vibrato aids their expression.

Orchestral bowing

Italians speak of the string section as "bow instruments," and they are closer to the truth by this terminology than we are with our emphasis on the mechanical vibration of the string. All expression on the instrument comes ultimately from the bow, and not even vibrato can overcome the defects of a tone that is faulty because of improper use of the bow.

The mistakes that are frequently made in working the bow using its full length are too numerous to mention. The student should check in a mirror periodically to see that his bow moves throughout its entire length in a straight line perpendicular to the string. The pressure of the bow on the string must be regulated by the first finger and the little finger using the thumb as a fulcrum. When the first finger presses, more pressure is added to the weight of the bow on the string. When the little finger presses, pressure on the string is less than the weight of the bow on the string. (See Figure 8–20.)

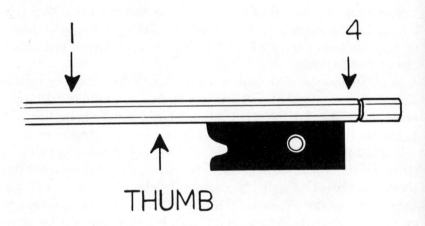

Figure 8–20: BOW PRESSURE CONTROLS
The thumb must be pressing up on the stick of the bow so that the amount of pressure on the string can be regulated by the first and fourth fingers of the bow hand.

Having the factors of direction and pressure under control, the student is ready to study bowing. If he plays long enough, he can discover by experiment what to do with the bow on each rhythmic pattern upon which he comes, but really, this is asking too much of the student—this subject can be taught. The great work of Samuel Applebaum in this area must be mentioned. His instruction books[1] make the study of bowing a systematic procedure which it never before has been.

Bowing can be explained as a matter of mechanical advantage. The wider the vibration of the string in the center, the louder the sound. Pulling the string with the bow near the bridge makes the string move farther in the center than when the bow is near the fingerboard. Therefore, a loud note or a very long note is easier to play near the bridge. Bow speed has much to do with the process. Extremely long notes or slurs simply cannot be played on a stringed instrument with a reasonable tone. Short notes cannot be played near the bridge with a full bow—a harmonic will speak instead of the fundamental; in other words, the string will squeak.

Some implications of the above principles are these: fast bows must be used near the fingerboard, slow bows near the bridge; loud short notes can be done with a fast bow near the fingerboard; very long notes need a slow bow close to the bridge.

The possibility of using a short bow for a short note is the other half of the bowing problem. It is the better way of handling a short note (rather than moving the bow suddenly nearer the fingerboard), but it is not always possible. For instance, continuous measures of half-note and quarter-note construction demand a slow, heavy bow for the half and a fast, light bow for the quarter. Only one other way is possible—put both notes in the same bow. This is often better, except at slow tempos.

The short bow is profuse with possibilities for most rhythmic patterns. A complicating factor is a long note among short ones. The long note must start at the frog or tip for best results. To bring this about requires much planning of, or changes in, the bowing of the notes immediately preceding the long note. To help in this matter, the teacher can plan the students' bowing for them and train them in acceptable ways of changing bowing.

The editing of the bowing in your students' music, therefore, is not just a matter of indicating up or down-bows. The size of the bow, the speed, the location of the bow on the string, what part of the bow to be used, and whether to bounce or stay on the string are all things that might require indication on the student's page.

---

[1]Published by Belwin, Inc., Rockville Centre, N.Y.

One way of accomplishing this editing is to mark the first chair player's part only and train the section to follow their leader explicitly.

Students are generally unable to make the bouncing bow sound well except near the frog of the bow.[2] Even there they are likely to lift the bow too far off the string, resulting in a *staccatissimo, pianissimo* passage. The bow must always remain close to the string. The volume of the bouncing bow stroke is increased by using more bow. In other words, the flatter the arc of the bouncing bow, the louder the result.

Students have trouble bowing a note on the string following one that was bounced. They throw the bow onto the string and try to draw it at the same time—of course, the bow bounces. It must approach the string horizontally in order to stay in contact with it. Slow practice in changing from the arc-like motion of the bouncing bow to the horizontal motion of on-the-string bowing is necessary. To learn to do this at a fast tempo requires much practice with emphasis on keeping the bow close to the string. The beginnings of both on and off-the-string notes must take place in the lower half of the bow when they follow one another.

Check to see that your students are not using too much tension on the bow hair. A bow that is too taut tends to bounce excessively. It also draws a glassy tone from the instrument.

Steps you can take in improving the bowing of your string section are: (1) teach the weight distribution of the bow with the thumb as a fulcrum and the first and fourth fingers as adjusters, (2) study Samuel Applebaum's books for a systematic approach to bowing problems, (3) analyze poor results in terms of the mechanical advantage principle in order to locate the cause of the trouble, (4) plan all important aspects of the bowing in detail, (5) teach the students to make changes in the indicated slurs of the music in order to bring about more artistic results, (6) guard against the development of a bouncing bow that leaves the string too far.

---

[2]*Spiccato* in the lower half of the bow is frequently necessary in orchestra. The *sautille*, a different kind of bouncing bow that takes place in the middle, is an advanced technique for which the short *detache* can be substituted. See: Ivan Galamian, *Principles of Violin Playing and Teaching* (Englewood Cliffs, N.J.: Prentice-Hall, Inc., 1962). p. 78.

9 PREPARING ORCHESTRAL WIND PLAYERS

As the director of the high school band is normally responsible for the training of all the players in his organization, so can the orchestra director reasonably be expected to train all of his students. Teaching all of the wind instruments is difficult, but interesting.

Students are always to be encouraged to arrange private lessons with an experienced performer-teacher. Even when this is possible, however, the school director still has the responsibility for training each player as he is performing in the orchestra. Part of this responsibility is to let each player know what musical skills and instrumental proficiency he needs to develop.

A wind player in an orchestra is at times a soloist, a member of a small ensemble, and a small part of the whole orchestra. Experience will teach him when to function in each capacity. His preparation in orchestral playing must include instruction to make him capable of all three types of playing.

Personality has much to do with the success of an orchestral wind player. An extrovert who is confident of his musical ability will have no trouble producing what is expected. An introvert who is overly cautious will have trouble balancing his sounds with those of the other players. The player's personality has a bearing on the type of instruction he should be given.

As a wind player enters the orchestra, he must have a background in playing that is more advanced than that of people in the string section. He must be able to play his part, relying on no other person for help. This is difficult, and it is often desirable to give support to the various sections by having reserve players to assist when needed.

The soloistic nature of orchestral wind playing

Solos within a composition should be played with the same force and skill as if the player were standing in front of the orchestra playing a solo. Even when the passage is not a solo for one instrument, each wind player is in effect playing a solo if no one else has his line of notes. This is different from a band where there might be six second trumpets, ten second clarinets, etc. The band conductor will spend rehearsal time with his second clarinets; the orchestra conductor will not want to spend any significant amount of rehearsal time with his one second clarinet. The student in orchestra must be able to keep his place and solve most of his problems in rehearsal without assistance.

There is an anonymity to playing second horn, second trumpet, etc. that some students like. Make them aware that they are not just harmonic support; they are soloists also. Especially when their rhythm is not like the melody, the part must come through, and they will have to play as loud as the player of the first part.

The ability to play a solo needs to be cultivated in every orchestral wind player. He can get experience from solos with the accompaniment of a pianist or a recording. Chamber music also gives soloistic training because only one instrument is on each part.

Playing solos and chamber music makes use of the techniques and notation that the player has been taught. Through this experience the player develops the necessary confidence in his reading that enables him to think beyond the mechanics of playing.

Instrumental proficiency

A player entering the orchestra will not have all the skills necessary to project his part firmly in all of the literature he will be asked to play. He will need further instruction and drill on all of the PRITT skills in addition to explanation of theoretical material, notation, and musical interpretation. The lesson format suggested in Chapter 6 is a very practical one for instruction of the wind players.

PHRASING

Watching a high school dramatic production can be a painful experience if the actors recite their lines without the proper expression. The same thing happens in a high school orchestra when the notes are played without the proper phrasing. The wind player must use his tongue, breath, and embouchure to give the required emphasis and shading to the notes.

A wind player's breath is similar to a string player's bow in that the faster it is used, the louder the sound becomes. *Crescendos* are produced by releasing the air faster and faster; *decrescendos* are managed by slowing down the speed of the air. Breath released too slowly will not support the tone, and the sound disappears.

The *forte-piano, fp,* is produced by fast air that slows down immediately after the beginning of the note. *Marcato* is similar, the difference being that the air slows down gradually for it. Another important aspect to *marcato* is the stopping of air between the notes. When the air stops, the pressure of the diaphragm muscle remains. This makes it possible to start another note without new impetus from the breathing apparatus. The throat acts as a valve in conjunction with the tongue.

Staccato notes are produced by pulsating bursts of air similar to *marcato*. In *staccato*, the note is cut short before the speed of the air lessens. Except at fast tempos, the tongue will come forward after each note in order to help cut off the sound. Diaphragm pressure remains during a *staccato* passage. This is particularly important in the typical French horn afterbeats—impossible if the diaphragm relaxes after each one.

The function of the tongue at the beginning of a note has seldom been described fully. Beginners are taught to move the tongue as if saying "Ta." This produces a *marcato* attack. An accent is produced by a tongue motion with a stronger T. Instruction past this point is necessary for other musical effects.

Legato attacks are accomplished by releasing the tongue gradually so that no burst of air enters the instrument. This is called

"soft tonguing," and the syllable "du" is usually associated with
it. If the "d" gets too hard, it makes a *marcato* attack. Some players get better results with "la."

All soft playing deserves the *legato* attack. A regular attack on
a soft note produces an accent; the attack is out of proportion
with the note. Also, full air pressure will produce a small accent
no matter how soft the tongue. Some of the air must be held back
until the tongue has moved away.

The register of the note has much to do with the tonguing syllable. High notes require that the mouth be closed tighter; the
vowel "ē" is put after the initial consonant for these notes (tē,
dē, lē). Low notes require the vowel "ō." Figure 9–1 shows the
change in the vowel of the tonguing syllable according to the register of the note.

Figure 9–1:   TRUMPET ARPEGGIO TONGUING SYLLABLES
**The vowel shapes the mouth cavity according to the note being
played. The "ä" is as in father, "e" as in ten.**

Staccato tonguing is usually described as if saying "tut." "Dit"
is a better syllable for many players. The throat cooperates with
the tongue, but this need not be pointed out to a student unless
he is getting an unusual sound at the end of his *staccato* notes.

In all tonguing, unsatisfactory results should lead a player to
search for a different syllable. Experimentation is the best method
for finding a syllable that produces the right effect. The various
formations of mouth, tongue, and teeth that are found in different
individuals precludes the possibility of determining what is right
for everybody.

When to take a breath is often a phrasing problem. Some players will breathe too often, others not enough. Breath should be
taken at phrase endings, whether the player needs the breath or

not. The task, then, is to get the students to identify the phrases.

Conducting motions can include signals for breathing. This teaches the phrase and at the same time insures uniformity of the release. A cut-off gesture with the left hand is a simple way to tell the players to end the phrase by taking a breath.

Signaling for phrase endings becomes impractical in polyphonic compositions. A signal for a breath in one part will create doubt about the phrasing in players of other parts. You may have to edit the important phrase endings in the parts. Otherwise, rehearse the melodies separately, signaling for breaths. Leave out these signals when the melodies are combined.

Sustained music that should not be interrupted by breathing is difficult for a young orchestra to play. It can be managed if reserve players are on hand to take over the melodic line from an out-of-breath player. Doing this smoothly requires a soft attack from the entering player.

Small breaths taken frequently can make a phrase seem somewhat sustained. It is a way of managing a passage of consecutive eighth notes. Another way is to make use of a reserve player. Without his help, the principal player may have to eliminate some notes. Even so, this is better than playing *sotto voce* because of a lack of breath.

The release of a note is important simply because it should be inconspicuous. An accent or change of pitch at the end of a note ruins a phrase. Students who make these unusual sounds can be taught to end notes properly. The breath support is suddenly, but gently, removed from the note. If there is to be a considerable silence before the next note, the tongue is positioned to prevent accidental sounds.

RHYTHM

Wind players who change the rhythm or tempo can lead the orchestra astray. Thorough rhythmic understanding and adequate technical proficiency will prevent this to a great extent, but the players need much experience in playing various rhythms in various tempos.

You can write exercises like Figure 9–2 to be performed by the student. Increase the difficulty, depending upon the needs of your players. Work on these exercises should proceed in four stages, each one having the beat more abstract. In the first stage, the student is directly involved with the beat by tapping his foot. Next, the metronome can click the beat. Then he should play from a conducted beat in strict tempo. If he has trouble, you can click the beat by letting the baton strike your music stand on the down-beat. The final stage is playing from a *rubato* conducted beat.

The most practical exercises for playing in rhythm are found in playing chamber music, solos with accompaniment, or duets with the teacher. Some of the most advanced rhythms are found in stage band music. Contrary to old-fashioned ideas, players can be helped by this type of music. Unfortunately, stage band orchestrations do not include parts for all types of wind instruments. Those players who can participate will learn much about rhythm.

INTONATION

All wind instruments must be prepared to meet the A-440 standard. Any that can't should not be used. Tuning to a different A would cause insoluble problems in most wind instruments. For the same reason, the rehearsal piano should be kept up to pitch. If the technician tells you it won't hold the pitch, that piano should be put in service where the pitch requirements are not so rigid.

Each instrument has some built-in intonation problems, and the players must learn to cope with them. The most troublesome of these notes are shown in Figure 9–3. Adjusting the instrument to produce these notes in tune would cause several others to go out of tune. The adjustment is therefore done by alternate fingerings or embouchure change.

Each player's chromatic scale should be checked against a tuning instrument, piano, or organ. The tuning adjustments should be made so that all pitches are within lipping distance of the correct pitch. You can expect that a severe embouchure adjustment will be necessary for the problematic notes discussed earlier.

As you check each player's scale, you may uncover other tuning difficulties. Young flutists tend to play flat in the low register and sharp in the high. Tune them on high notes, since that's where the flute plays. A wrong adjustment of the cork in the head joint will cause the high register to be out of tune. Oboe and bassoon players depend upon the reed for their intonation. A poor clarinet

Figure 9–2: COMMON RHYTHM PATTERNS
This exercise is only a simple scale repeated over and over, but the rhythm of each measure is different.

Figure 9–3:   PROBLEMATIC NOTES (CONCERT PITCH)
These are the notes that frequently cause tuning problems in full orchestra chords.

reed can adversely affect the intonation of that instrument. Lipping notes higher is impossible on the clarinet. This fact recommends setting the tuning adjustment a trifle high so that no notes are left flat. Various fingerings are possible in the high register; the player should learn the ones that give the best intonation on his particular instrument.

Alternate fingerings are possible on the French horn, especially the double horn. Some fingerings are better in tune than others, but the fingering also affects the tone. The fingering with the best tone that is closest to being in tune is the one the player should use. Experiment extensively with the placement of the valve slides. Octaves differ, so you must tune more than twelve notes.

Trumpet players can solve some of their problems if their instrument has a first and/or third valve trigger to extend the slide when necessary. Alternate fingerings help on certain trumpets.

Trombone players must be taught which notes to humor with the slide. Checking the overtone series in all seven positions will show the player which notes need to be adjusted in which direction.

Tubaists share the flutists' inclination to play sharp on high notes and flat on low ones. Tune the tuba on low notes, since that is where it plays. A fourth valve eliminates the need for the troublesome 1-3 and 1-2-3 valve combinations. Pull the fourth valve slide until the low C is in tune.

Technique

Once the player has the correct fundamental approach to his instrument, he is ready to develop his technique. Tonguing, fingering, breath control, and embouchure control are all involved in technique study along with reading skill. The teacher serves to program studies for the student in each area, and also to guard him against developing bad habits.

You can correct a student's approach to the instrument if his bad habits are not too firmly ingrained. Make sure that the habits are indeed bad ones before you try to correct them. Remember that different physical characteristics necessitate different approaches to an instrument. Observe as many professional players as you can to see different successful approaches to the various instruments in matters of embouchure, posture, finger position, etc.

One of the technical accomplishments students are anxious to make is a complete mastery of the range called for in the orchestra music. The very high and very low notes may confuse a student because he doesn't encounter them often enough to become familiar with them.

Flash cards can be made to teach new fingerings—the note on one side and the fingering on the other. The student can make these himself; check to see that he has copied the fingering correctly from the fingering chart.

New notes can be taught one at a time in a familiar song transposed into new keys. (See Figure 9–4.) The player will be able to tell by ear if he has a wrong fingering.

The same type of study can be used to help brass players develop greater range. The high notes are physically difficult to play because the embouchure muscles must hold the lips together while the air being expelled tends to force them apart. A player can take advantage of this air pressure by wedging the lower lip inside the upper. The air will help to push the lower lip against the upper. (See Figure 9–5.)

After the high note study similar to Figure 9–4, further control of brass high notes can be gained by the practicing of études containing them. A violin book would serve for trumpet players, cello studies for trombone, and bass studies for tuba. Scales that extend beyond the normal range can be practiced, the theory being that a player who can play high F won't be afraid of high C.

Low notes are a problem for horn, trombone, and tuba. A study introducing one low note at a time can be written, reversing the procedure of Figure 9–4. Scales extending into the lower range should be practiced. Some of the technical problems can be simplified on the trombone if it is equipped with an F attachment, and on the tuba if it has a fourth valve.

Tonguing fast notes is a technical problem. Double and triple tonguing are used on the flute and all brass instruments when the speed is too great to tongue the notes regularly. Start students double tonguing by having them practice repeated notes alternately tonguing one and starting the other with the throat (an action similar to a cough). Have them accent the second syllable to make it have a definite beginning: "ta-KA." As the speed increases, the accent will disappear, but the clarity will remain. Speed in double tonguing can be gained by saying two words aloud faster and faster: "duck, a." Triple tonguing is used for triplets in the same manner: "ta,ta,ka" on brass instruments, and "ta,ka,ta" on flute.

Transposition is a technical problem on some instruments. The first step in teaching it is to provide the student with a knowledge of key signatures, scales, and the piano keyboard. Clarinet and

Figure 9–4:   OBOE HIGH NOTE STUDY
Each transposition introduces another note of the high register.

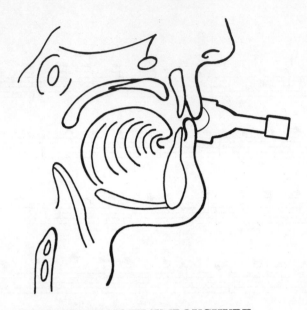

Figure 9–5:   BRASS HIGH NOTE EMBOUCHURE
The position of the lower lip can be arranged to make the production of high notes easier.

horn players must think of transposing "Clarinet in A" and "Horn in E" parts not by flatting each note, but by playing one scale degree lower than each written note, in the key a half step lower. (See Figure 9–6.)

On the Steppes of Central Asia (Borodin)

Figure 9–6:   CLARINET IN A TRANSPOSITION
The B-flat clarinet player must think of the notes of his part (below) as he plays a part written for clarinet in A. The F horn player does the same transposition when playing parts written for horn in E.

A student who is scale-oriented to transposing will have no trouble except with accidentals placed in front of the note. The procedure for playing these is to alter the note in the direction that the accidental changes the note from the written scale. (See Figure 9–7.)

Figure 9–7: TRANSPOSING ACCIDENTALS
The note of the scale the player is thinking must be altered in the same direction that the accidental alters the note of the original key signature.

TONE QUALITY

A good tone is one that is rich in overtones. For instance, the best flute tone is one that sounds least like the pure tone of its relative the recorder. Instruments naturally sound richer when played loudly; the student must learn to keep the sound rich as the volume decreases. The long tone study and the *crescendo-diminuendo* exercise described in Chapter 6 will help.

Many people search for the ideal mouthpiece and the ideal instrument. Though these might be worthy pursuits, most of the young student's time should be spent learning how to operate the equipment he has. Assuming the instrument and mouthpiece are of standard quality, the student can learn to produce a tone that will be characteristic of the instrument. The lack of ideal equipment can become an excuse for lack of effort. Instruments purchased for the school should be of proven quality so that you can be sure that substandard results are the fault of the student, not the instrument.

As an instrument changes the part it takes in the musical texture, it also changes tone quality to some extent. An extreme example would be the different tone colors a saxophone would use in playing the melody in Richard Rodgers' *Slaughter on Tenth Avenue* and blending with the French horns in Prokofieff's *Lieutenant Kije*. Incidentally, the saxophone should be played with a sub-tone on auxiliary parts that are added to the original. The support that they give the strings may be welcome, but the tone quality shouldn't attract attention.

The necessary change in volume from solo to *tutti* playing usually brings with it enough change in tone quality that one player will not stand out from the group. The thing to be guarded against is a player that stands out from your orchestra like one fine voice in an amateur choir. Each player must know when to project his line with full richness and when to hold it in with the other players, no matter how weak they are.

VIBRATO

In Chapter 8 it was pointed out that even a poor vibrato from a player helps the string section—not so the wind section. A poor vibrato is distracting in any of the wind instruments, particularly on a solo. Vibrato makes an unskilled player sound nervous. An audience listens to a solo passage like this tensely, in fear that the player will not make it to the end of the solo. It is better that the player play without the vibrato if his is distracting. In fact, the oboe, bassoon, saxophone, trumpet, trombone, and tuba sound quite musical without vibrato, even on a solo part. Clarinet and French horn never need it, and the flute needs it only on a solo.

If you want to teach your wind players to vibrate, get some advice for teaching it from a good player of each instrument. Of course, it would be preferable to send each student to this player to learn vibrato and other ways of enriching his tone. In lieu of such a player, you can use the advice found in books and periodicals.

Reserve wind players

The ideal orchestra rehearsal would keep everybody busy; therefore, it is not good to have many players on reserve. Yet, depending on one individual is dangerous. If he becomes ill or breaks a finger the day of a concert, you won't have a trained player for that part.

It is impractical to include a reserve player for every part. Seating them in the orchestra would separate those players who should be beside each other for good ensemble. If you were to permit these extra people to play all the time, the orchestra would take on a band sound. Another consideration is that it would require much of your time to train all those additional players. Then too, more players cause more problems in attaining ensemble.

Following are listed some practical reserve players to have on hand, along with some suggestions for making good use of them when they aren't needed to replace an absent member.

1. A third flute player plays piccolo or third flute when necessary. He can double the second part on *tutti* passages, thereby strengthening the naturally weaker lower notes.
2. A third clarinetist can play bass clarinet or double the second part on *tutti* passages. If bass clarinet is important in most of your music, you may want to have a fourth player in the clarinet section.
3. The third oboist can play English horn when the score calls for it. He can relieve tired players or take over if a player has to adjust a reed. Doubling either oboe part is likely to overbalance the other winds.

Reserve brass and percussion players should be on hand according to the orchestration of most of the music you're using. The player of the second part should be considered a reserve player for the first part. Have them switch places in rehearsal occasionally to make sure the first part can be covered in case of an emergency. One possibility is scheduling reserve brass players on a part-time basis. You could rehearse the numbers calling for them on the certain days of the week when they would be present.

Maintenance and repair

An instrument in need of repair will not let the notes speak in time to provide good rhythm. Technical passages will be blurred. The tone will be substandard.

The student may blame himself instead of the instrument when he can't play a part. He may even develop bad playing habits in an attempt to make the malfunctioning instrument work. It helps if you can test the instrument by trying it yourself. If not, have the player try another instrument to see if he has the same difficulty.

Brass instruments develop problems due to dirt, corrosion, dents, and other effects of wear. However, even an instrument fresh from the factory can cause trouble. A slight leak in a woodwind will not cause problems at a slow tempo, when the player has time to press on the key. In a fast tempo the affected notes will not speak because there is no time to press.

You can help the repairman by telling him which notes are out of order. It isn't necessary to locate the cause of the trouble. Leave it for the repairman to find. Blowing smoke through the instrument or pressing down hard on woodwind pad cups can cause damage.

Several books are available that tell you how to do emergency repairs. This is fine if you are only going to do them in an emergency. It is a waste of your time, however, to repair instruments that a professional repairman could fix in his well-equipped shop in a fraction of that time.

THE
10 PERCUSSION
SECTION

A large part of the excitement of a piece of music is due to the percussion part. It adds rhythmic pulse, coloration, and dynamic emphasis. Because it has such a profound effect on the music, it deserves much of the conductor's attention.

A superficial glance at percussion technique makes it seem easy. Many teacher-training institutions neglect it by having no percussionists on the staff. Anyone who has studied with a percussionist knows that the technique is not easy, and anyone who hears a school orchestra perform will almost certainly find fault with the percussion section.

Orchestral percussionists must have attributes that fit their special task. Once the right players are selected, they must be provided with the proper equipment and instructed in its care. Instruction in playing includes the same PRITT skills as for other players, but the lesson procedures must be adapted to provide for instruction on all the various instruments that a percussionist is expected to play.

The percussion player

Each member of the percussion section can be trained to be a thorough musician. He can learn to play all the color instruments, the sound effects, the drums, the tympani, and the keyboard instruments. Learning all this makes him capable of playing the percussion part to any composition you might want to use.[1]

The percussionist is a musician whose specialty is rhythm. Aptitude tests that measure ability to remember and reproduce rhythmic patterns are appropriate for evaluating your prospective percussionists. Besides a good sense of rhythm, the ideal percussionist would have vitality, patience, curiosity, attentiveness, and a desire to perform the music exactly as it should be.

A player trained to specialize on one percussion instrument will spend his days in orchestra like an actor in the wings waiting to go onstage. Trained on every percussion instrument, he can become thoroughly involved in the music.

Percussion equipment

The size of drums is measured in depth and diameter. Thus, a 14″ x 28″ bass drum would have a shell fourteen inches wide and twenty-eight inches in diameter. This size is adequate for an orchestra; anything less would be designed for dance band use. The same applies to a snare drum 8″ x 14″. The diameters of the normal pair of tympani are 25″ and 28″, 23″ and 30″ the diameters of the third and fourth.

All drums need tension screws to adjust the tone of each head. This means that double tension is required for the bass drum, tenor drum, field drum, tom-tom, and snare drum (side drum). Adjustable tension is also a desirable feature on the drums with one head: conga drum, timbales, bongoes, and tambourine. It is indispensable on the tympani.

The keyboard percussion instruments that are called for in orchestral music are: chimes, marimba, xylophone, orchestra bells, celeste, perhaps vibraphone, and the piano and harpsichord if you wish to consider them percussion instruments. All are rated in number of keys or octaves of range. Anything less than two and one-half octaves is substandard. Three octaves is normal for the vibraphone, and three and one-half for the xylophone and marimba.

---

[1]Watch for Kenneth Mueller's forthcoming *Teaching Total Percussion*, Parker Publishing Company, West Nyack, New York.

Cymbals come in light, medium, or heavy weights. Light weight hand cymbals (crash cymbals) are in danger of being turned inside out; heavy ones exhaust the player. Ones larger than eighteen inches are too heavy to manipulate using the leather handles that are best. Twenty-two inches is a good diameter for the suspended cymbal that is struck with a beater. Struck with a stick it is called a ride cymbal.

Other cymbals are called for occasionally. Antique cymbals are thick plates of brass that must be struck with a beater. Tiny finger cymbals are struck against each other with the finger and thumb of one hand. An elastic band straps them on. Hi-hat cymbals are twelve or fourteen-inch cymbals mounted on a stand equipped with a foot pedal that opens and closes them as they are struck with a drumstick. A gong, called tam-tam in scores, is suspended from a cord and struck with a beater.

The triangle is an important percussion instrument. Aluminum or steel triangles range in size from four to eight inches. They need not be struck with the beater supplied; sometimes a large triangle struck with a small beater is just the sound you want. Other instruments that are struck are: the cowbell, the wood-block, the anvil, and the Chinese temple blocks.

Instruments not previously mentioned that are needed for Latin-American music are: the guiro, chocallo, cabaza, maracas, and claves. Spanish music calls for castanets. A spring-mounted set permits finger articulation that is best.

Novelties, and even some serious music, call for sound effects such as: boat, bird, or song (slide) whistles; animal calls, ratchet; thunder or wind machines; bicycle or auto horns; sandpaper blocks, and the slap stick (whip). An easy way to purchase these is when they're needed, since most are inexpensive.

Accessories are needed to make the various instruments play-able. The weight and length of drumsticks affects the sound. Various models should be supplied. Roll them on a flat surface to check for straightness. Bass drum beaters and tympani mallets come in lamb's wool or felt. A double-ended bass drum beater makes a roll possible using only one hand. Tenor drumsticks covered with lamb's wool can be used for striking the suspended cymbal as well as for playing the tom-tom and tenor drum. Other accessories include wooden bass drum beaters, wire brushes, timbale sticks, a beater for the gong, a mallet for the chimes, and various beaters for the triangles. Keyboard instrument mallets should be on hand in yarn, plastic, and varying hardnesses of rubber. Brass mallets are available if you care to have them used on the instruments. The sound is brilliant, but they do put visible dents in the bars.

Stands are needed to support the instruments for playing: bongoes, timbales, snare and bass drum, temple blocks, bells, tomtom, gong, and suspended cymbal. Holders are needed for triangles, the cowbell, and the woodblock.

You can have the school purchase some equipment each year until the percussion section of the orchestra is supplied with the instruments needed. Good equipment will last many years with proper care. (See Figure 10–1.)

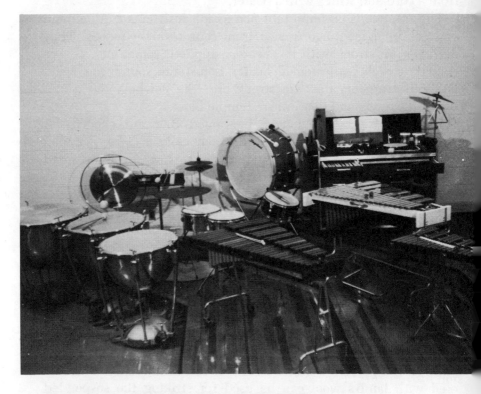

Figure 10–1: PERCUSSION EQUIPMENT
     Some of the equipment shown has been in use over ten years in the Fisher Junior High School Orchestra, Ewing Twp., Trenton, N.J.

A percussion cabinet provides storage for all the traps. It helps the players to organize their equipment, and it protects the equipment against would-be drummers who are likely to break things. Many drawers are helpful, and a lock is necessary. Figure 10–2 shows a percussion cabinet that incorporates a trap table, music rack, and cymbal holder.

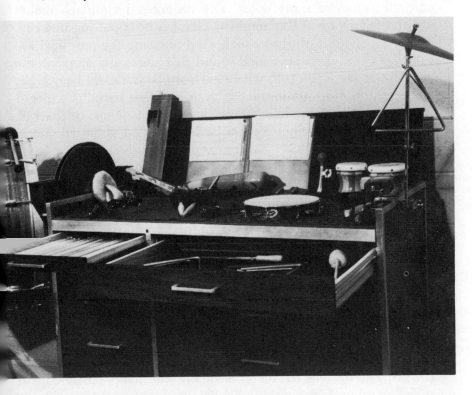

Figure 10–2: PERCUSSION CABINET
All equipment is instantly accessible in a cabinet such as this one by Wenger Corp., Owatonna, Minn. Photo by the author.

Percussion PRITT skills

The control of all aspects of performance is possible on percussion instruments. The methods of control and the type of training necessarily differ from the other instruments. The multitude of percussion instruments, each having different techniques, makes it impossible to explain here how they are all controlled. Following are the items that are important for the high school player to know in order to play musically in orchestra, taking for granted some background in the fundamentals.

PHRASING

The roll is a way of sustaining a note on the instruments that can only produce short notes. The rudimental approach makes the student aware of the number of strokes he is putting in a roll. This type of roll can distort orchestral phrasing. The musical approach is to make a sustained sound that starts and stops at the right time. The open roll, where each stroke is clearly heard, has a different musical significance than the buzzing sound of a closed roll. The speed of the hands determines the closeness of the roll, and it is an expressive factor similar to the speed of the vibrato in other instruments.

The degree of shortness of notes can be controlled to some extent on certain of the percussion instruments. Using one hand for a damper can shorten notes of the drums, suspended cymbal, and bells. Playing near the center of a drum also makes the notes more crisp. Conversely, long notes are played halfway between the rim and the center.

Accents are produced on percussion instruments by using a higher than normal stroke. Even when accents are not indicated, the normal metrical accent is made by a stick slightly higher than normal. This is an element of playing that makes a drummer sound musical, not mechanical. For instance, the stick pattern of triplets should be high, low, low. Normal alternation makes this Rlr,Lrl. This accents the meter normally and makes possible great speed with perfect rhythm. Rrl,Rrl produces another phrasing and Rll,Rll still another. Certain passages may lend themselves to one of the latter stickings. (See Figure 10–3.)

Sticking can do much to change the phrasing of a passage because the sound of the instrument being struck repeatedly in the same place is not the same as when it is struck in different places for consecutive strokes. An obvious example is the Indian drum beat: Rrrr sounds like the Indian drum, and Rlrl sounds quite different. This is one reason the technique of reserving one hand for each of the tympani doesn't produce musical results. Proper phrasing is accomplished by turning toward the tympano in use and alternating sticks.

RHYTHM

Perfect control of rhythm is expected of a player, but it can't be taken for granted. It only comes when the player has adequate technique, good equipment, and is sensitive to the motions of the conductor and the sounds of the other orchestral musicians.

Wrong entrances are a frequent mistake caused by the long rests in percussion parts. It is a good idea to write in what is going on at each rehearsal letter during a long rest. Cued notes in the part near the end of a rest will also help. A cue from the conductor will prevent players from missing an entrance; mark your score so you remember to give it.

A conscientious percussion player can develop rhythmic problems, as anybody can, by listening to the orchestra in order to determine his rhythm. In doing this, he is reacting to the sound that he hears, and he will be late on each beat by the amount of his reaction time. These players must be taught to react to the sight of the conductor's baton and not to the sound of the orchestra.

Players with a fine rhythmic sense can cause trouble with the tempo by trying to control it too rigidly. They start, say, at a tempo of M.M. 96 and the rest of the orchestra starts at M.M. 90. After five seconds they are a half of a beat apart, the percussionists trying to pull the orchestra along, and the rest of the players thinking the drummers are rushing. The only solution is to train the percussionists to follow the conductor's beat even if he changes tempo.

Poor sticking can make playing certain rhythms difficult. The sticking problem corresponds somewhat to the bowing problem that stringed instruments have with certain rhythms. A good example is the rhythm featured in Beethoven's *Seventh Symphony*. Figure 10–3 shows the bowing and sticking that get best results.

The analogy of bowing and sticking is often valid. One instrument, the sandpaper blocks, can be played exactly as a bowed instrument. The left hand block is held still and the right hand block "bows" it. Even the "bouncing bow" is possible; the arc must be kept very low to avoid knocking the blocks together.

Figure 10–3:   BOWING AND STICKING ANALOGY
The solution to a rhythmic problem by changing the bowing may
also solve the problem for percussion.

INTONATION

The tympanist is the only percussionist who has to match
pitches. Tuning on the other instruments is a matter of adjusting
tone.

The pedal can be used to adjust the pitch once the fundamental
note is set by using the tension screws. This is easily done if the
pitch is identifiable; simply loosen or tighten the screws until you
have F on the 28″ tympano and B-flat on the 25″. If the head is
out of tune with itself because some tension screws are set higher
than others, the tympano will sound like a bass drum. You will
not be able to identify the pitch.

A singable pitch must be obtained by adjusting the tension
screws. Test the pitch by striking the head about three inches
from each screw. Adjust the screws around the head several times
because the whole head is affected by the turning of one screw.
A normal stroke about five inches from the rim will produce
acoustical beats if the head is almost in tune with itself. Some
small adjustments should remove them, and you can set the desired pitch by moving all tension screws an identical amount.

If the tympano is so far out of tune with itself that the above
procedure won't work, complete retuning is necessary. Loosen all
tension on the head, then tighten each screw to the point where
it is ready to start pulling on the head. From here tighten each
screw the same amount until an identifiable pitch is obtained.
Make this pitch identical around the head before bringing it up
to the fundamental tuning note.

The pitches called for in the music can be obtained by use of the pedal. Depending on the humidity, a good cowhide head can be raised as much as a sixth from the tuning note. It is difficult to stop the pedal on the exact pitch. The sensation is somewhat like tuning a chrome-steel string with the tuning peg—any motion up or down is too much. Practice is necessary to gain the necessary control of the tuning pedal.

When lowering the pitch, either by pedal or screws, the player should always take the slack out of the head by pressing on the center of it. Otherwise the slack will come out during playing, resulting in a flat pitch. The final adjustment can be made after the slack is pressed out. This adjustment should always be upward in pitch. In fact, every pitch should be approached from below to avoid the problem of slack in the head. If the tympano is tuned to C and you want to change it to A-flat, go to G first and then come up to A-flat.

Changing pitches during a piece must be done without playing. Players do it with their ear close to the head, stroking it with a finger as if striking a match.

The chromatic pitch pipe is the most convenient reference for tuning the tympani. Players depend less on it as they gain experience. Their knowledge of scale structure and interval relationships lets them tune the tympani to any notes, once the fundamental tuning notes are set. Much of this knowledge they gain from the pitch pipe. The difference in octaves and tone quality may cause beginning tympanists to have trouble tuning the tympani with the pitch pipe. The singing voice can serve as an intermediary between them. If the player sings the pitch of the tympano, he can easily determine what is wrong by contrasting the sung pitch with that of the pitch pipe.

A final adjustment may be necessary as the tympanist begins playing. This must be done carefully between notes so that no glissando is heard. Since the tympanist is acutely aware of the process of matching pitches, he should have no trouble knowing when an adjustment is necessary. Experience will teach him when to try to adjust and when to leave well enough alone.

TONE

The tension on the head largely determines the tone of a drum. Many books prescribe a note to which they should be tuned. This is only a basic guide, a general pitch area, not an exact note that would be dissonant in chords where it didn't fit.

The pitch level of the bass drum should be adjusted to be below the bass staff. If a definite pitch results, detune the drum by alternately tightening and loosening tension screws around the head. The snare drum also must be out of tune with itself. If it is in tune with a certain note, it will sing by means of sympathetic vibrations every time that note is played. Even if it is properly tuned, forced vibrations from a loud sound will make the snares ring; they should be released to avoid this. The player must mark in his part "Snares off" at the beginning of a rest and "Snares on" at the end of it. A professional example of bass and snare drum tone unaccompanied can be found in a recording of Kodaly's *Háry János Suite*.

The tension of the snares is an important factor in the tone of a drum. Set it by adjusting the tension screw on the snare strainer. Put the lever in "on" position and set the screw so the snares are lightly touching the bottom head. Keep playing the drum with one stick as you tighten the screw. The tone will gradually get better until the snares become too tight.

Tympani tone is largely determined by the material with which the heads and mallets are made. Plastic tympani heads have overtones that are objectionable on the larger tympani. You must decide whether the easier maintenance is worth the sacrifice in tone. Felt heads on the mallets get a powerful, rhythmic, percussive sound. Lamb's wool heads produce a *legato*, rich tone. For a glassy, *staccato* passage, try xylophone mallets.

Playing technique greatly influences tone. The sounding spot at which instruments are struck is very important. The grip on the striking instrument and the angle of it as it hits also affect the tone. Unsatisfactory results will lead you to ask your players to change one or more of these things to try for better tone.

The gong is played with a large lamb's wool beater. The spreading splash of sound is more effective if the player sets the gong into motion beforehand. Tapping the edge lightly causes a vibration that can be felt but not heard. A gentle stroke near the center produces the sound.

The crash of the suspended cymbal is made by a strong stroke of a small beater near the edge. No warm up is necessary.

The tone of the woodblock is best when it is struck near the center, somewhat closer to the open side. The shoulder of a snare drum stick can be used, but a bell mallet insures a consistent tone. Mounting the block on the frame of a drum amplifies the percussive sound. It is better to have it held by the edge, mounted on a special stand, fastened to the percussion cabinet, or resting on the trap table. In the latter case, felt pads must be glued on the corners to raise the center off the table.

Claves are played with one hand cupped underneath one of the rosewood sticks to serve as a sounding chamber. This stick is struck in the center, directly above the sounding chamber, by the shoulder of the other stick.

TECHNIQUE

The technique of drumming is usually thought of as a study of the twenty-six rudiments. These apply to drum corps playing, but only a few basic ones are needed regularly in orchestra. Great fluency with these is necessary, however. The single stroke, the long roll, the flam, the flam accent, and the ruff occur in the music at all tempos.

The single stroke must be studied for matched tone of both sticks and perfect control of rhythm at all volumes. The accent should be studied in conjunction with it. Studies accenting every other stroke, every third, fourth, fifth, and sixth stroke are easy to memorize but hard to play. Combinations of these are extremely difficult as the tempo is increased. (See Figure 10–4.)

Figure 10–4: SINGLE STROKE ACCENT STUDY

All but one of the accents work out to be alternate sticks. On the repeat the sticking automatically reverses.

The long roll must be steady with all strokes equal in volume. It is best practiced on a drum with gut snares or even a practice pad; wire snares cover up much unevenness in a roll. The technique of ending the roll must be studied. A roll tied to a note has a firm ending. A roll that is not tied has a final stroke no louder than the notes of the roll.

Consecutive flams at a fast tempo are difficult, but otherwise they are no problem. Flams in combination with single strokes form the rudiment of the flam accent. It has two forms, one with a single stroke between flams and one with two single strokes between them. Both require much practice to gain facility. The student must also be fluent with the combination of the two. (See Figure 10–5.)

Figure 10–5:   THE FLAM ACCENT
Three different heights of the sticks are necessary to play the flam accent. This exercise should also be practiced with the sticking reversed.

The three-stroke ruff is just a flam with two grace notes instead of one. It is no special problem, but the four-stroke ruff is. Three soft, single-stroke grace notes followed by a normal stroke require delicate control and fast hand action. (See Figure 10–6.) The five-stroke roll is an easier substitute.

Figure 10–6:   THE RUFF
The double strokes of the three-stroke ruff are played with a bouncing stick. The four strokes of the four-stroke ruff are single and traditionally always lrlR.

Tympani technique is different from that of the snare drum. A drummer learning tympani must learn to do the single stroke roll. Then he must learn to manage playing on two or more tympani besides learning to tune them.

Passages are smoother if there is a minimum of crossing one stick over the other. Many times this can be avoided by advance planning. An uneven number of pick-up notes into the new pitch should start with the stick on the tympano where the pick-ups are located. An even number should start with the stick that will play the other pitch. (See Figure 10–7.)

R   L R L   R   R L R L   R   L R L   R

Figure 10–7: TYMPANI STICKING
The stick used should be in the direction of the tympano with the desired pitch, as in this example. Reversing this sticking would be clumsy.

The crossover technique is required on the keyboard percussion instruments, and no amount of planning can eliminate it. A technique not used on the tympani, crossing under, is necessary on the keyboard instruments. Experimentation will enable you to find a sticking for a keyboard passage. As on all percussion, sometimes the best solution to a problem is to use the same stick twice in a row.

Cymbals are difficult instruments to control. A crash can be prolonged by holding the cymbals high and turning them toward the audience. The cymbals can be damped against the player's chest to end a tone. At fast tempos, one side can be left there while the edges away from the player are opened and closed to make the sound. There is not the usual up and down motion in this case. An alternative is to have one player hold the cymbals together while another strikes them with a soft stick.

An important part of cymbal and trap technique is to set them down without sounding them. An ordinary music stand with a solid desk covered with felt will serve, but a trap table is preferable. It can have slots cut in it to hold the cymbals.

Percussion lesson procedure

Because of the many instruments to be covered, continuity of instruction is hard to maintain in percussion lessons. An ideal lesson would include hearing and assigning a drum study, a keyboard study, a tympani study, and a trap study. This would be in addition to rehearsing orchestra music and a percussion ensemble. Since this ideal lesson would take more than one period, a more practical lesson has to be developed.

The typical percussion lesson can include a drum study, orchestra music, and a percussion ensemble. The percussion ensemble and orchestra music would include trap instruction and keyboard work. Each player can play a different instrument on repeated performances of the same ensemble.

Scale practice and exercises based on scales can be played on the keyboard instruments by the class. A small set of bells can be signed out by the students for practice at home. The rest of the percussionist's keyboard practice will have to be done in school.

Scales on the tympani teach the location of all notes. The rest of the class can play the keyboard instruments as the tympanist tunes. He will see how much pedal adjustment is necessary for whole steps and half steps. Exercises in fourths and fifths such as Fussell's *Ensemble Drill*, pp. 30–31, will provide more typical practice in changing the tuning. The tritone that occurs in each key (ti-fa) will be an unusual tuning for the tympani, but it is used in some modern compositions.

The percussion lesson should be planned to increase the PRITT skills of the players on all percussion instruments. Because of limitations of time, the lessons will necessarily concentrate on those skills and those instruments that are most in need of improved performance.

Maintenance

Cowhide drum heads shrink in dry weather. If the drum (especially tympani) is loosened daily to lower it to the proper playing pitch, the collar of the head will disappear. When this happens, the drum will no longer be tunable. Moisture can be put back into the head to regain the collar. Place wet towels on the head. When it begins to sag, tighten the tension screws. Repeat the process if necessary. Replace the wet towels with damp ones and permit the head to dry gradually.

Bongos and other drums with no tuning screws can be lowered in pitch by the foregoing procedure. They can be raised in pitch by using a flame to dry out the excess moisture in the head.

Tension on drum heads should be adjusted on a dry day. Heads tightened when the humidity is high may split when the humidity returns to normal. Keep all drum keys in your possession so you will know when the heads are being tightened. Keep all drums away from sunlight. The collar on the tympani heads can be preserved by leaving them tuned to a high note, except on damp days.

You may have a snare drum that rings like a bell after it is hit. Eliminate this by installing a muffler inside the drum that can be adjusted by a screw on the shell. If this internal tone control isn't adequate, a thin strip of cloth stretched inside the head will help. (See Figure 10–8.) The cloth inside the drum is not to be confused with the felt cloth placed on top of the head to produce the muted sound called for by the word *coperto*.

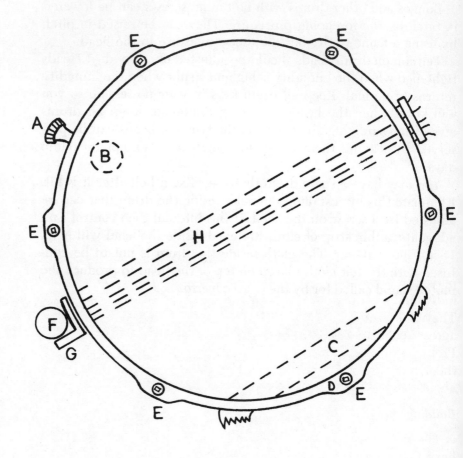

Figure 10–8: SNARE DRUM MUFFLERS
  A. Internal tone control adjustment screw
  B. Internal tone control muffler under batter head
  C. Cloth strip muffler under batter head
  D. Counterhoop
  E. Head tension screws
  F. Snare tension screw
  G. Snare release lever
  H. Snares under snare head
The mufflers do not interfere with the playing area of the head.

11 PROBLEMS OF ENSEMBLE

The effectiveness of the music played by an orchestra depends not so much upon the skills of the individual players as upon the blend that they achieve as a group. They can make a good impression with only average skills if they agree upon rhythm, tempo, phrasing, intonation, and balance. Problems arise in reaching this agreement in all five areas. Solving them requires constant searching for procedures that will bring about the best ensemble of which the students are capable.

Building ensemble

The best way to improve the way players play together is to have them play together—each passage over and over again. The drill is repetitive and tedious. What saves it from becoming boring is the improvement that occurs.

Drill cannot be productive unless understanding precedes it. For example, if you want certain notes of a passage shortened, the students must know which notes are involved before they can begin to agree upon the shortness of them. This type of understanding is imparted by careful instruction and demonstration.

Instruction given during the drill is usually limited to pointing out progress. Areas that are better can be mentioned along with ones that need further improvement. When progress ceases, the drill should be ended for that day. Once the students get the idea of playing in rhythm, keeping the tempo, matching the phrasing, adjusting the pitch, and contributing the proper amount of sound, less drill will be needed.

Chamber music makes the players aware of ensemble. The woodwind quintet in the center of the orchestra will blend better if they know each other's playing from ensemble experience. The brass section will play orchestral passages together better if they have played brass compositions often. The principal string quartet will match bowings easily if they are used to it from playing string quartets.

Rhythm

Rhythmic problems are the most serious ones that an orchestra can have. Wrong rhythms blur a passage, and the people who play them are likely to lose their place in the music. Since it is of such importance, rhythm is the first thing to unify in rehearsal.

Three activities that precede rhythmic drill are explanation, demonstration, and trial. The trial tells you if the explanation and demonstration have been effective. If not, a different explanation is in order. Explaining in a different way is necessary; the students won't understand if you simply repeat the old explanation. After a successful trial, the drill for perfect rhythmic ensemble can begin.

What you would really like to do with a rhythmic problem is point to the notes on each student's page as you demonstrate. If you anticipate a problem, you can make a chart of the rhythm to use as you demonstrate. Notate the rhythm without a staff so that readers of different clefs can be equally at ease reading it. Add arrows to indicate the beats of the measure. Point to each beat as you demonstrate vocally. Demonstrate to each side of the orchestra to make sure all can see the chart.

For a rhythmic problem you didn't anticipate, you can write the rhythm on the chalkboard or try teaching it without a chart. You may postpone work on it. If only one player is involved, you will want to work out the problem in his lesson. One person having trouble with a rhythm can prevent others from learning it. He can help by remaining silent as you work on it with the orchestra.

In demonstrating, there is little to be gained by restating the wrong rhythm that has been played. Learning cannot be derived from contrasting the sound of two rhythms unless the players can see both written out. If you do contrast rhythms, let the correct one be the last the students hear you demonstrate. Drill them on it until they have completely forgotten the wrong rhythm. This is the point of the sample lesson in Chapter 5 dealing with the triplet figure.

Playing a rhythm on concert A is a good transition from the explanation to the performance of a rhythm. It will be easier for the students to concentrate on the rhythm when they don't have to read pitches. After ensemble is attained using concert A, the passage can be rehearsed using the printed notes.

Rests within a passage cause more trouble than continuous notes. Anxious players shorten the rests and finish the passage too soon. Cautious players wait too long for the rests and end up late. The passage must be analyzed for the players so that they know when to play according to the conductor's beat.

Passages with complicated rhythms can be worked out a measure at a time. Putting the measures together can be troublesome; after each measure is learned, drill it with those already learned.

Books are available for full orchestra that emphasize rhythm. You can find rhythms in the book that correspond to the problem at hand. The presentation in the book will be more repetitious with fewer tonal problems. This simplified presentation will prepare the students for the problem in the orchestra music.

Tied notes are often troublesome—more so in orchestra than for individuals. Players are reluctant to hold the note when they hear other parts moving. Show them how their part fits with the others. They can then judge the length of the tied note by ear.

Wind players having a long note tied to a short one can rest on the short note in order to breathe. This is an acceptable way of phrasing the passage, and it gets the rhythm played correctly.

Ties involving short notes can be worked out by having the players intentionally disregard all the ties at first. Then rehearse with an accent on the notes at the beginning of each tie, but still articulating each printed note. Finally, add the ties and remove the accents. (See Figure 11–1.)

Syncopation is a rhythmic problem that involves ties. The technique of disregarding ties at first will help in teaching many syncopated passages. Syncopation is often written out without ties,

Figure 11-1:   TIED NOTE PROBLEM
Rehearsing rhythm a as shown in lines b, c, and d leads to a correct performance, e.

however, and other methods of working it out are necessary.

Simple syncopation involving only eighth and quarter notes can be taught by the "Morse code method": eighth notes are short and quarters are long. "Short, long, long, short" is a measure of simple syncopation in $\frac{3}{4}$.

Thorough understanding of a syncopated rhythm requires that it be related to the conductor's beat. Always include baton motions with your demonstrations. To emphasize the relation of the syncopated notes to the beat, let the baton click each beat by touching your music stand.

If you want to make the analysis of a syncopated passage perfectly clear to the orchestra, you will need a teaching aid. Charts, projected excerpts, recorded examples, or a rhythm demonstrating machine might be used.

Syncopated entrances can be explained to students as a reaction to the beat. Accent the stroke of the baton after which they are to enter. They will soon learn to wait for this accented beat. You will be more comfortable giving the cue with the beat rather than after it.

The quarter-note triplet is difficult to play evenly. It can be explained as a form of syncopation. (See Figure 11–2.) When the student can space the triplet over two beats while tapping his foot, he has it under control. Until this is accomplished, he must think in cut time, tapping the foot on only the first note of each quarter-note triplet.

Figure 11–2:   THE QUARTER-NOTE TRIPLET
The technique of disregarding ties at first helps in teaching this rhythm. Tapping the foot on each beat is to be advocated.

An uncommon meter signature can be explained to the students by relating it to one they understand. For example, $\frac{9}{8}$ can be related to $\frac{6}{8}$. In lessons, give the students a chance to practice figuring out the beats. This will also serve as a test to see if they understand the meter thoroughly. Use a dittoed sheet as described in Chapter 6. Have advanced students write their own rhythms in the meter being taught.

Complicating factors of tempo, phrasing, and technique can

delay your work toward rhythmic ensemble. Rhythm cannot always be the first thing unified. Judge what aspect of playing is farthest from good ensemble, and work on it first.

Tempo

The ensemble disappears when some sections of the orchestra rush or slow a tempo. This is a serious problem that deserves much rehearsal time. The only solution is to develop in the students more sensitivity to the playing of the other people and the baton motions of the conductor.

Most problems occur because the students are concentrating so hard on playing the notes that they don't notice they're straying from the tempo. Passages that present the most challenge often are rushed because of the anxiety the players have about them. If this happens, explain that since they are playing it faster than it should go, they have no reason to worry about it. Ask them to concentrate on tempo as you drill them on the passage. The repeated experience of playing it together cures much of the anxiety and worry that the players feel.

Drill on a technical passage can be a systematic procedure. Rehearse the parts one note at a time if necessary. Then take them in rhythm at a slow tempo. Next, combine the parts and work for facility by gaining speed on each repetition.

The speed that students are able to work up to on the technical passages has a bearing on the tempo of the whole piece. If they can play the difficult parts even faster than your ideal speed, you can feel safe in using the proper tempo. If they can't approach this tempo in the technical passages, you have the choice of letting the passages be blurred, slowing down for them, or slowing the whole piece. You might choose to do some of each.

Phrasing affects the tempo. For instance, young players don't want to be silent between *staccato* notes. They rush into the next note. It is necessary to have them mentally subdivide the beat so that they play during one half of the beat and rest the other half. A *staccato* passage can be rehearsed slowly with a subdivided beat of the baton as a preparation for this kind of thinking.

In rehearsal, as you call attention to the details that should be improved, the tempo will naturally become slower. The players will take time to be careful and evaluate their playing. Since these things are desirable, it is reasonable to sacrifice the tempo. It can be brought back as you review the piece.

It is difficult to obtain good ensemble at a slow tempo. The slow beat of the baton confuses the players. For this reason, many school conductors divide the beat in slow passages where a professional would not. Repeated rehearsals of a slow composition, a few minutes each day, help the ensemble.

Balance

A player sitting in the orchestra hears a sound that is by no means the balanced sound heard by the audience. A classic story is told about a bass player from the opera orchestra going to the opera on his night off and hearing the melody for the first time. The story has an element of truth in it, because every player is so close to his own instrument that the sound of it almost fills his ears.

A player learns to play in proper balance from following the example of his fellow orchestra members and the requests of conductors. A young player soon learns that the dynamic markings in his part are a rather unreliable indication of the volume required. Later he learns how his instrument sounds as a part of the background for an oboe solo, as a part of the melody, as a part of the harmony, as a part of the full orchestra, etc.

Errors that distort the balance will have to be pointed out to the students. If one player is standing out from his section by using excess volume, he must bring it down to the level of the other players. Perhaps the other players are playing too softly, but the thing that is important is that they all agree, so that the effect is not that of a solo instrument playing with orchestral accompaniment.

Brass and percussion players have difficulty assessing the volume they are producing in relation to the orchestra. The bell of a trumpet above the music stand will cause the trumpet sound to dominate the orchestra; to the player it will be no louder than usual. A stroke on the snare drum from a height greater than eight inches is a severe accent. Most playing is done within two inches of the drum head.

Balance is greatly altered for the players in the transition from rehearsal room to the auditorium stage. The playing sounds completely different in these two situations, and everyone has to get used to it. In fact, from one auditorium to another the balance appears to be different. Also, the erection of an acoustical shell on a stage that had none previously will affect the way the players hear themselves in relation to the others. Young players are quite surprised by the change when they move into a new situation. For this reason, several rehearsals in the concert setting are needed to help the players be at their best.

Phrasing

The phrasing should be learned along with the notes as much as possible. It is not easily added after a piece is learned; in fact, it is almost impossible to change the players' way of thinking about a piece once they have it learned.

A recording used to introduce a composition demonstrates phrasing. The students will copy this phrasing. If you want to make a change, it will still be easier than to try to bring together several different versions.

Your demonstrations to correct the rhythm of a passage can include phrasing. Notes you want accented or shortened can be demonstrated that way.

You can also help players to phrase together by the way you conduct. The left hand is especially useful for this because it is free to move without affecting the rhythmic beat of the baton. Tiny cut-offs given with the left hand signal the release of notes. It can also signal *crescendos, diminuendos,* accents, and *staccato.* The baton can also indicate some of these phrasings. It must be used when the left hand is busy giving cues or adjusting the balance.

Edited parts help the players to phrase together. Marks can show them what special emphasis to add, where to breathe or lift the bow, when to stand out, and when to play under the volume of another instrument. Words can be inserted into the parts to indicate phrasing of a passage: *marcato, legato, staccato,* etc.

Certain effects will be remembered better if you just tell the player what you want. If you want the last note of a recurring melody to be cut short, it is much easier to tell the players than to put the necessary dots in every player's part.

Often you will want to discuss the phrasing. Sometimes it is linked to a special idea the composer wanted to get across. If so, the players have to know what they are expected to do. For example, a drum passage of sixteenth notes won't sound like gunshots unless the player phrases it that way.

How live the auditorium is determines much about phrasing. A large accent in a live auditorium has an echo that disturbs the music that follows. In this type of auditorium the volume should be less, the accents underplayed, the separation of notes exaggerated, and the tempos slowed.

Accents are special phrasing problems because they have to be prepared. The drumstick has to be raised, the tongue has to be put into position, the bow has to be pressed into the string. These preparations necessitate an instant of silence before the accent is played.

The opposite of an accent is *legato*, and it is more difficult for young players to produce. The ideal *legato* attack produces a note with no initial emphasis—the tone is suddenly present with no *diminuendo* following. This is the sound a conductor wants when he asks the orchestra to sound like an organ.

The release of a note is important because it should be uniform. Rehearsal is necessary to have all players agree just when to release each note.

Theoretically, a whole note is supposed to last until the first beat of the following measure. This is not normal playing technique, however, and if you want a note at the end of a phrase sustained full value, it should be marked with a *tenuto* sign, the players should be told about it, and you should conduct it with the left hand raised, palm up.

Bowing

Some directors go to great lengths to achieve uniform bowing; others disregard it completely, letting the players take care of it. The musical results will indicate how much you need to work on bowing. Since it affects the phrasing, it is certain to need attention at times.

Uniform bowing is generally desirable with a school orchestra because there is so much difference between the sound of a young player's down-bow and his up-bow. The down-bow is strong, suited to accents and loud beginnings. The up-bow is adapted to soft beginnings and *crescendos*. Smooth playing is better in the upper half of the bow, loud playing in the lower half.

The part of the bow to be used, the length of the stroke, the proximity to the bridge, the pressure of the bow on the string, and the direction of each stroke are all things that can be matched to make a passage effective. Drill is certain to be required, regardless of the amount of editing that has been done in the parts.

Drill on bowing should be begun by perfecting the intonation. At first bowing is disregarded as you strive to have the players match pitches. When the passage is ready to rehearse slowly, explain the bowing to be used. Of course, it will be ineffective at a slow tempo, because the amount of bow that gets best results at a fast tempo will be insufficient at a slow one. After the bowing is uniform, the passage can be drilled progressively toward the proper tempo.

Except in complicated passages, the bowing can be left to the principal string players. The others can follow to bring about uniform bowing within each section. You can rehearse the principal string quartet, perhaps with the principal bass added, so that they agree to bow together when they're playing the same rhythms. Most bowing work on the orchestra music can take place in the string orchestra rehearsal.

Intonation

Even when adequate tuning procedures are used, the ensemble will not automatically play in tune. Good intonation is a fleeting thing with school players; it's there one measure and gone the next.

When a new instrument takes over the melody, the supporting players will adjust their pitch level to match it. This happens even in professional orchestras, and it is not of great consequence when the error is small. When the error is large, as it often is with school players, the supporting players become confused.

The solution to the pitch level problem is to choose a more reliable guide than the melody instrument. It must be an instrument that plays almost all of the time, and it must be audible to all players at all times. The bass is ideal. It meets the above qualifications, and the small number of players will have few disagreements in pitch among themselves. If your bass section includes inexperienced players, you can check the tuning of their strings and permit them to use open strings freely. Unless the players are truly erratic, the bass section will maintain the pitch level and serve as a reference for all the instruments.

The most difficult passages for intonation are those in unison. Nobody knows whom to match. You can take one section of the orchestra or a keyboard instrument and have the melody played note by note. The rest of the players join in softly and match pitches with each note. Another technique, if the intonation is generally correct, is to have the orchestra sustain each note until agreement is reached. Both techniques naturally require drill as a follow-up activity.

Tone color

The matching of tone color is important in the string section. Bowing is the key to it. If a passage of eighth notes is bowed by the first violins using ten inches of bow and by the seconds using five, the tone color of the string section won't be unified, even if the players do manage to match in volume.

In general, a richer tone is obtained by using more bow. Young players will have difficulty using the necessary fast bows and keeping them on the string. They will do better in the upper half of the bow, using adequate pressure of the first finger.

Asking for a richer tone requires that you be permissive about bow changes. The rich tone uses up the bow so fast that long slurs will have to be broken. In certain passages where you want a sustained rich tone, you can teach the students the technique of staggered bowing. If each player changes direction at a different time, the new attack will not be heard, and the tone will be enriched by the faster bows.

Vibrato makes the string section have a lively sound. The first task is to get all players to use vibrato. If you are lucky enough to have all players that vibrate, you can work on the intensity of the vibrato for the tone you want in certain passages. Varying the width and speed of the vibrato changes the expression of the note being played.

12 THE CONDUCTOR'S PROBLEMS

Every conductor is both a musical leader and a teacher. Regardless of the skills of his players, the better he teaches and conducts them, the better they will play. He will try to bring forth the music from his players according to the way he believes it should be played. How well he succeeds is a measure of his effectiveness.

The study of conducting is often thought of as learning the proper motions to use. Though this is important, it by no means insures good results. True conducting is shaping a musical performance. All subjects that bear on this are pertinent to the study of conducting. The musical preparation, teaching techniques, and even the personality of the conductor are involved.

The conductor's personality

A conductor must inspire his players to perform well. This is almost automatic when you are genuinely interested in teaching an orchestra. Your enthusiasm will be contagious; your players will be eager for rehearsals and performances.

Your enthusiasm will be dampened if you expect too much. Demand good playing, but acknowledge to yourself that daily improvement is all you can realistically expect. The thrill in teaching comes in helping students achieve today what they couldn't yesterday. Ask for much, but expect little. Praise correct results and improvement, and work on problems systematically to enable improvement to take place.

An objective attitude toward the playing is necessary to bring about the best results. The ear of a school orchestra conductor is assaulted with so many wrong sounds that it is in danger of becoming dulled. He may get so used to poor rhythm and intonation that he doesn't notice them. You can guard against this by listening the way you would to a professional orchestra. Of course you will find a myriad of errors, but then you can work on the glaring ones first. Encourage your orchestra with remarks about the improvements being made. Confidence will grow in the players as they improve, and then you can ask for more.

An objective attitude is hard to maintain. At times it may seem that students are purposely making the same mistakes over and over. The cause of repeated mistakes is insufficient knowledge and/or skill. Maybe you haven't explained well. Perhaps there is a misprint somewhere. In any case, emotional outbursts on your part will not help the orchestra play better. You will be discouraged when a certain mistake is made right after you've tried to eliminate it, but control your temper.

Conducting motions

The motions necessary to communicate clearly with an orchestra are more varied than the diagrams in conducting manuals would lead us to believe. Each phrase of a piece requires different motions to signal cues and items of phrasing that go far beyond the fundamental beat pattern.

Many of the motions necessary to make your interpretation clear to the orchestra will come to you naturally. Others will require practice. Few people think of conducting as an art that requires manual dexterity, but it does. Hours can be spent on your podium in front of the empty chairs of your orchestra. This is score study and conducting practice combined.

Practicing your conducting gives you perfect control over your interpretation. Practice to give cues on time, to indicate dynamics, and to include all preparatory beats. Never lose sight of the musically satisfying interpretation you are trying to form. You shouldn't slow down at difficult spots just to get a better look at the score. A metronome will tell you if you are doing this. Practice at slower tempos and increase your conducting technique gradually. Once you have the technical mastery to conduct even faster than the proper tempo, you can turn off the metronome. Then you can interpret as you wish, with the knowledge that you are slowing down in certain places according to your interpretation and not due to a lack of conducting skill.

Skill can be gained by practice, and it is worthwhile so that you won't have to think of your conducting technique while rehearsing your orchestra. Your thoughts can be on what the players are doing, what they should be doing, and how you can get them to do it.

It may occur to you to practice conducting with a recording. When you do this, you are reacting to the sound of the orchestra on the record, trying to match your downbeat with their playing. If you practice this, you run the risk of following your own orchestra in the same way. As a conductor you are a leader, and the orchestra must react to your beat.

The importance of the preparatory beat cannot be overstressed. The height of it indicates dynamics, the sharpness of it shows the nature of the attack, and the speed of it shows the tempo. When the music starts differently from what you intended, suspect your preparatory beat of being faulty.

Players must be trained to follow the preparatory beat. The time between the preparatory beat and the downbeat sets the tempo. You can emphasize this fact by starting the same piece at different tempos. Also try indicating different attacks and dynamic levels from the ones printed in the music. This training in following a conductor is needed by the players.

Giving cues is a technical problem for the conductor. They can be given with the baton, the left hand, or a nod of the head. In any case, there should be a preparatory indication to enable the player to prepare his note.

Giving cues with the baton distorts the beat pattern unless the instrument to be cued is in the direction of the beat being given. The left hand can cue if it is not needed to indicate dynamics. To give a cue with either hand, raise it in the direction of the player just before the downbeat of his cue.

A nod of the head is an effective cue. It holds the advantage of freeing the hands for their usual functions. Looking at the player ahead of time serves as the preparation and the nod as the cue.

Your conducting motions indicate to the players how you want the notes played. Nothing is more ridiculous than the conductor shouting "Piano!" while his baton is waving like a buccaneer's sword. Dynamics can be indicated by the size of the beat pattern. Students will follow this indication better than those printed on the page, if they are trained to do so.

The lack of response of a school group may lead a conductor to enlarge his baton motions in an effort to whip the sound from the players. Besides being a considerable physical effort, this leads to a beat pattern that isn't clear. A beat at the conductor's knees is not visible to the players.

A tired conductor also develops an unclear beat. Good conducting posture can help to prevent this. The strong back muscles do some of the work if the arms are in a position with the elbows away from the body. A grip on the baton similar to that of a tympani mallet is comfortable. The back of the hand is toward the ceiling, and a small beat can be given with only wrist motion. Only an extremely large beat requires any motion of the upper arms; the forearm is adequate for almost any beat.

Slow tempos are tiring to conduct. The slow motions of the baton are also difficult for the players to follow. A note that is supposed to be exactly in the middle of a beat can easily be miscalculated. Subdivision of the beat can ease this problem and help to make the tempo clear. Keep the main beat large and the subdivision small so the people who don't need the subdivision won't be confused. Beating a measure of eight as two measures of four will confuse everybody.

Many conductors have trouble with fermatas. The problem is in resuming motion after the fermata. A preparatory beat must be given in order to do this. You can solve the problem by sustaining the fermata with the left hand, thereby freeing the right to give the preparatory beat anytime you choose. There are three basic choices you can make: (1) the music can start immediately after the fermata with no pause at all; (2) the preparatory beat can be simultaneous with the cut-off of the fermata, resulting in a short silence after the fermata; (3) the fermata can be followed by a long silence. The left hand raised, palm up, will sustain the sound. You can turn it over for the cut-off after the preparatory beat has been given (as you would in choice number one above); at the same time as the preparatory beat (as in choice number two), or before the preparatory beat (choice number three).

The preparatory beat after a fermata should be in the direction of the beat before the one on which the motion resumes. If the fermata is on the third quarter note of a four-beat measure, the third beat will have to be repeated as the preparatory beat.

Helping uncertain players

Special, unorthodox motions can help players who are having trouble understanding what they are supposed to play. The rhythm of their part can be dictated by the left hand of the conductor. One case where this is helpful is the quarter-note triplet. The baton keeps the pulse while the left hand dictates the triplet. The problem in dexterity this poses for you is worth overcoming if it helps your students to get the feel of the triplet.

When players tend to leave a note too soon, you can keep them on it by keeping the left hand raised. Dropping the hand indicates they should leave the note. This is helpful in the case of a long tied note. Hold the note with the left hand and indicate the end of the tie by a sharp cut-off gesture. The players will release the note on the cut-off and start promptly on the notes that follow.

Baton techniques can be altered temporarily to explain rhythm. A mechanical beat with a sharp motion at the top and bottom can be used to indicate the beat and the middle of it. This makes the placement of off-beat notes clear. In conducting the finished product, this subdivision must be discarded in order to keep the tempo. Off-beat notes are the responsibility of the players.

Dictating notes with the baton may be used as a teaching technique. As a conducting technique, it is not very clear. To be successful, every dictated note needs a preparatory beat. Otherwise, the players are only guessing when the baton will strike the bottom of its arc.

Much of the inexperienced player's uncertainty about when to play can be removed by the explanation of baton motions. The players must be shown what you mean by the downbeat at the beginning of every measure. The beat that leads into a new measure can also be shown easily, because it, too, looks the same no matter what the meter.

Most baton motions will become clear to the students as they are used. The players don't have to know the details of how you will conduct each fermata; what is important is that they respond correctly.

Unusual motions may call for an explanation. Try the passage first; your motions may solve the problem before it exists. If you talk about the problem first, the players will look for something unusual and perhaps do something unnatural. Following your conducting will be easy and completely natural if the motions are clear.

In problematic spots, the best thing you can do is follow the suggestion given in Chapter 5: be consistent in your motions. If you conduct a spot the same way each time, the players will soon figure out what you want.

Teaching players to be alert to your conducting during the progress of a piece is not as easy as getting their attention at problematic spots. They will watch you closely at beginnings, fermatas, and endings, but they also need to observe your tempo and phrasing constantly. One technique that develops this attention is purposely distorting the music. Change dynamics and tempo, signal for breaks in the middle of phrases, and insist that your players follow. Upon repetition of the passage you can conduct normally, and you will find the players more responsive.

Maintaining a strict tempo is often impossible in a school orchestra because of the limitations of the players. Many times you will acquiesce to the tempo fluctuations of the players in rehearsal. This helps them to learn the piece. Later though, you will want a steady tempo. Check yourself by having a flashing metronome (with the sound turned off) at the back of the room. You may be surprised at the amount of fluctuation you've been permitting.

Learning the score

You can gain familiarity with a composition by playing it as a member of an orchestra or by listening to a recording. Either way you get a good basic introduction to the melodies, rhythms, and harmonies that you would otherwise have to figure out for yourself. You will save time if you have this knowledge of a score you plan to use.

True knowledge of a score, however, can only come from studying it, vertically and horizontally, so that you know what is in it. When you study this way, you are forming your own interpretation of the work, not copying that of another conductor.

Study a score generally at first. Get an overall idea of the message of the piece, the tempos and the climaxes. Plan the phrasing of the melodies and the dynamic relationships between them. Learn the distribution of the parts on the page and get acquainted with the orchestration.

Getting down to specific items starts with learning anything in the score that is unfamiliar to you. Check the background of the composer to learn something of the style with which his music should be played. The style of performing associated with the period of a composition is a part of the learning you want to transmit to your students.

The meaning of the words in the score should be double-checked to make sure you know them. You could assume that *clarini* in the score meant clarinet if you didn't look it up. You might assume that *Hörner in B* meant your F horn players would have to transpose the distance of a tritone unless you were aware that the German B means B-flat, and H means B-natural. More of this type of information may be important to make a proper interpretation and correct performance possible.

Study the musical content of a score with the intent of learning everything in it. After studying it, you will want to be an expert on the rhythms, melodies, harmonies, form, and orchestration the composer used. It is not enough to be able to detect wrong notes. You will want to notice missing notes, out-of-tune notes, and those that are out of balance. Players can make other mistakes that are hard to detect because they are not exactly wrong notes. For instance, players may play cued melodies, percussionists may use the wrong instrument, and brass players may make harmony not in the score by playing in the wrong register. The students will expect you to detect this type of mistake, also.

Studying for melodic content is a matter of investigating every note of each player's part. Anticipate problems that you will have to solve in rehearsal. Plan the phrasing carefully. Make sure to use the proper tempo for this. A phrasing that is effective at a slow tempo may be impossible at the proper tempo. As you study more of the parts, note carefully their relationship to the ones you have already studied. Plan the balance you wish to have between all the parts. Knowledge of the formal structure of the piece will enable you to decide which parts should come through and which should stay in the background. Remember to mark the cues that you will want to give to bring the various melodies in on time.

You will detect a wrong note in the full orchestra easily if you recognize it as being foreign to the harmony. The harmonic structure of the piece should become evident as you mentally superimpose the parts you have studied. A few chords may require investigation at the piano, but unless you are a pianist, using the piano may be only a waste of time. Exceptions are modern compositions where the harmonic idiom is complex.

Mark beats in your score for complicated rhythms so that you will know where in the measure to expect the notes. Any rhythm complicated enough to cause you to do this will be puzzling to the players. Make a chart to help you explain it.

The form of the piece determines much about the expression to be used. The excitement that tempo and dynamics can give should be planned. It may be a good idea to tone down the beginning so that the end can be more impressive. You might decide to alter the dynamics of a repeated section to avoid monotony.

You should have an overall plan of interpretation in mind. The danger in studying each measure is that the message of the piece may be lost. As you spend your days working out the details of a composition, don't lose sight of your overall plan.

A score need not be memorized. Your brain is busy enough without this extra strain. Partial memorization is inevitable as you study, though, and this is good. You can communicate better with the players through eye contact. You can evaluate the cause of their mistakes better if you watch them play. Eye contact is especially important at phrase beginnings and endings. The middle of a phrase is a good time to check your score for the phrase to come. Players are more careful when the conductor watches them. A good rule would be: "Never get caught looking in the score." The better you know a score, the less you have to look at it.

FULL SCORES VS. CONDENSED SCORES

Some numbers that you will want to use are published with only a condensed score. This makes teaching difficult. You may spend a whole rehearsal trying to find out who is supposed to play which notes of your score. You can avoid this by examining each person's part and marking your condensed score fully, adding notes where necessary. Use different-colored pencils to make the voice leading clear. A serviceable score can be made in this way, and you will be better informed after examining each part.

Full scores are best to teach from, but they are cumbersome to use in performance because of the frequent page turns necessary. A sensible plan is to use a full score to teach the composition and a condensed score to perform it. If you decide to do this, practice with the condensed score to get used to it before the performance.

Even when you have a full score, take time to examine a few parts to see that they agree with the score. Check that the arrangement matches your score. If the parts disagree with your score about rehearsal letters and measure numbers, change your score. Evaluate the legibility of the parts, and make a notation in your score where players have to read poorly printed music. This will tell you why the players are having difficulty in that spot.

Professional improvement

Improving your skills will lead to better results and more personal satisfaction. Evaluate your weaknesses and work on them. Don't forget that you need to be prepared both as a musician to judge performance and as a teacher to train students to perform better.

To see yourself as others see you, you might make a videotape of yourself in rehearsal. You will find much to object to when you watch the playback. Don't rationalize the mistakes you see on the tape; excuses are easy to make, but they won't teach your orchestra. Immediately change things you find wrong with your conducting and rehearsal technique. Then prepare a videotape of what you think is a good rehearsal on your part. Show this to colleagues and/or professional musicians. Consider their advice carefully.

An open mind is necessary if you really want to improve. Talking to other teachers and musicians can give you new insights that may prove to be valuable. Books such as this one and those listed in the bibliography can give you new ideas about music, about teaching, and about teaching music, all three of which you deal with daily.

Conferences sponsored by colleges, music dealers, instrument manufacturers, and music teachers' organizations provide opportunities for you to meet the people who are vitally interested in the music curriculum in our schools. At these meetings you can ask how others solve the problems you face. Make it a point to discuss these problems with the people you meet. The professional players at these conferences are often handicapped in their discussions by a lack of questions from the audience. This results in a lecture that deals with advanced problems that have limited application to school orchestra players. As you're teaching, certain wrong sounds will come from a student's instrument that you will be unable to correct. Take a written description (maybe even a tape recording) of these occurrences so that you can ask the people who may know the answer. You can also ask these professionals how to teach an aspect of instrumental technique that you can't get across to your students. Tonguing on the wind instruments and vibrato on strings are examples of topics that could be used for a full clinic session if you can ask the right questions. Take a list along. Take the same list to another conference and get different people to answer.

No matter how good your undergraduate training was, you will feel deficient in certain areas that are important to your teaching. Remedy this by taking graduate courses. Different teachers will give you additional insights.

Obtaining an advanced degree is becoming almost a requisite in teaching today, and you can learn much while doing it. You may feel the pressure to select courses you will do well in, rather than those you need to better yourself as a teacher. If so, you may have to postpone taking the courses you really want until your degree is completed.

The music teacher, especially a teacher of orchestra, has more opportunities for in-service training than any other teacher. When you listen to the radio, you may learn something that can be put to use in school. This is especially true of stereo FM programs, but you needn't disregard completely the music you will hear on T.V., in department stores, in the dentist's office, etc. This type of music will occasionally be part of your course of study if you really want to give your students a well-rounded orchestral experience.

Playing in an orchestra is a very valuable experience for somebody who is conducting one. Play under as many conductors as you can, and study their techniques. Adopt their successful procedures, and avoid the unsuccessful.

Live performances are an inspiration that you need frequently to remind you of the proper sound in a concert situation. Many teachers get so busy conducting and performing that they never get to a live performance. This leads to a lack of perspective in their thinking. We should often see an exhibition of the kind of performance we are trying to produce with our students. A major artist or symphony is not necessary for this. Much can be learned from a performance that is not perfect. Certainly you will be interested in seeking how concerts in other schools compare with yours.

Further study of your major instrument is an excellent way to improve yourself as a musician. A conductor is primarily an interpreter, using basically the same thought processes as when playing an instrument. It helps to have several teachers in order to get different outlooks on musical interpretation, teaching methods, and music in general.

Growth as a teacher is also important. Take advantage of the visiting day that most school districts permit. Visit a school with a thriving orchestra program. Your principal can arrange this for you if you don't know the music teacher of the other school. There is no better way to learn to be a better teacher than watching an experienced person in action.

Since an orchestra is mainly strings, you will want to improve your string teaching, no matter what your major instrument is. The summer conferences sponsored by the American String Teachers Association enable you to do this economically. At one of these conferences you can hear lectures and recitals by renowned string artists and teachers. You will meet other teachers of orchestra, and you will see some teachers working with adult and student string orchestras. All of these people are anxious to answer your questions and talk about orchestral string performance.

The steps you take toward professional improvement are certain to help you teach your orchestra better. You will feel more able to cope with the problems. You will be more certain of the music you prepare. You will find your job of teaching orchestra more interesting every day.

13 USING TEACHING AIDS

Anything a teacher uses to get a point across is a teaching aid. A teaching aid makes use of one or more of the senses of sight, hearing, and touch. The machines you studied in your course on audio-visual aids are teaching aids, but so are many other things, some of them quite common.

Teaching requires communication. It is impossible to communicate ideas without a medium. The spoken word, baton motions, facial expressions, and hand gestures are the aids every conductor uses in teaching his orchestra. The vocal demonstrations he uses are yet another kind of teaching aid. The chalkboard, electronic tuner, a piano, and a metronome help the school orchestra conductor to communicate better. The tape recorder is another aid that can be used to illustrate a point.

Teaching instrumental skills in lessons requires even more aids than those that help so much in orchestra. The ones listed in Chapter 7 are available commercially, and others can be made. A library of aids can be built up of materials that prove useful in presenting the subject over the years.

Properly used, a teaching aid makes your teaching efficient, it adds interest to your lessons, and it makes the learning permanent. The proper aid can give insight into a subject. Any means to give the student a clear concept of how the music is to be played is a welcome aid to the conductor. The better the understanding, the better the performance will be.

When you have a lesson in mind for a certain class, you will plan for the teaching aid that will do the job best. The aid you want may be too expensive or too much trouble to prepare, considering the importance of the point to be illustrated. Knowledge of the various aids will enable you to substitute an acceptable one.

The full orchestra itself is a teaching aid when you use it to explain musical points to an audience. In such use, the orchestra serves the whole student body of the school system.

It is important to use the aids effectively. They cannot communicate ideas—they only help. The teacher is more important than ever when a teaching aid is used, because he must explain what the aid shows. When you use an aid, your explanation of it (and the mechanical operation, if any) must go smoothly.

Effective use of teaching aids

Learning takes place when a person is prepared to learn from an experience, undergoes the experience, and makes use of the knowledge he has gained. Preparation for the use of a teaching aid should show the student how the aid fits in with what has gone on earlier in the class. He must be alerted to what he is expected to learn from the aid—how it will help him to understand a subject or improve his playing. Activities after the aid has been used should make use of the learning. Immediate application of the new knowledge will make the experience memorable.

Even a simple aid such as a demonstration needs this format in order to be successful. Consider the common occurrence of a section of the orchestra playing a wrong rhythm. You need an aid immediately to teach the correct version. Words are a logical first choice. If they fail, they have at least served as a preparation for a demonstration. A vocal demonstration is a readily available teaching aid. After the presentation, the follow-up activity is to drill the orchestra on the correct rhythm. No doubt you've been using this procedure so often that you take it for granted, yet there are conductors who haven't mastered this simple teaching procedure. I once saw a conductor ask for a note to be shorter, without saying which note or which instrument, and then proceed without having the orchestra play the section again.

A more complicated teaching aid requires one more step: the preparation of the aid itself. For instance, a movie has to be ordered and previewed. A projector and screen have to be obtained for the time the film is to be shown. Perhaps a projectionist must be secured to set up and show the film. The other steps (preparation, presentation, and follow-up) are the same, though of course they will be proportionately more extensive due to the more complex aid. The students have to be prepared for the many things the film will show. The follow-up of the film should also cover all of the same points.

Choosing a teaching aid

When the students' performance indicates the need for a teaching aid, the one that best would fulfill the objective should be chosen. Sometimes a simple drawing on the chalkboard will suffice. Other times it may require a movie, several recordings, some still pictures, and a demonstration to put across a single concept.

The teaching objective determines which aid(s) would be best. Convenience and time are considerations. The best aid may be a field trip to see a professional orchestra play. If this isn't feasible, you'll settle for a movie or a recording. Lacking these, you may simply describe to the students what they would have seen and heard in a live performance. The learning that takes place using each of the above aids is different. Which aid you will choose depends upon the importance of the objective as well as the availability of the various aids that could accomplish it.

Ideally, you will be able to select the aid you think is best for the purpose. Limitations of time, finance, and availability may force you to choose a substitute. The following descriptions will help you. The advantages and disadvantages of each are discussed, not to discourage the use of any one aid, but to point out the special characteristics that make each aid good for some purposes and not good for others.

Words

Ideas have always been communicated largely by words. They are used in conjunction with every other teaching aid. In fact, most aids are worthless without words to explain their significance.

In all explanations, use words that the students understand. You can teach new words by connecting them to a familiar subject: you can't teach a concept new to the students using words that are also new. Attach new words to a concept only after it has been learned. Asking a young orchestra to "observe the *Da Capo* at the end of the exposition" will earn you many a blank stare.

The special terminology of music should be used freely to acquaint the students with the terms all musicians understand. Esoteric terms can be omitted, but the common Italian terms should be taught. The best way is to explain them once and use them frequently to keep the meaning fresh in the minds of the students. Conducting gestures will remind them of meanings they tend to forget. In fact, it might be said that all foreign words in the music mean one thing: "Watch the conductor."

The written word is a substitute for the spoken word. Much can be learned about music and performance from reading. A book is a sort of portable teaching machine. Make sure you know what books about music are available in your library. You might make an annotated bibliography to let the students know what is there of interest to them.

DEMONSTRATIONS

This traditional method of instruction is still valuable. There are many times when the student will understand how to play his part only after seeing and/or hearing it done.

In lessons where you can take the students' instrument and demonstrate, you will frequently want to set the example for him. This method can be overdone to the point that the student gets discouraged; many teachers have the least success teaching their major instrument. Let the demonstration be a last resort in this case.

In orchestra you will be using time by taking up an instrument and demonstrating. You also run the risk of setting a bad example when you pick up a cold, untuned instrument and attempt to produce a polished sound. If you often feel the need to demonstrate instrumentally, use your own instrument, have it tuned, keep it within reach, and warm up before the rehearsal.

Vocal demonstrations are convenient. Even bowing can be demonstrated somewhat by singing while bowing an imaginary instrument. No matter how little vocal technique you have, you will be able to get most points across by singing. Singing along with the orchestra is rather useless, however, and it can turn into a bad habit. You can't hear what the players are doing while you're singing.

Demonstrations of a musical process can help students to form new concepts about playing. One example is the process of matching pitches. A demonstration of how one pitch is put into agreement with another by manipulating the finger, embouchure, or other tuning mechanism can start a student on the road to improving his intonation.

Demonstrations aided by words alone cannot explain everything you will want your students to understand. The main disadvantage is that the student can't feel, hear, or see it as the demonstrator does. Other aids can help the student to do this.

CHALKBOARD

The chalkboard is always near. On it you can exaggerate reality and exclude all distracting elements. A drawing can show the position of a clarinet mouthpiece inside the mouth, for instance, which could not be shown in a demonstration.

A process can be shown on the chalkboard. The relationship of key signature to finger placement on the fingerboard of a stringed instrument can be shown. Parts of this diagram can be erased and changed to show how a change in key signature affects the finger placement.

Drawings that you will want to make often can be painted on the chalkboard. Light lines can be painted as guidelines, or bold, permanent ones can be used. You can make a staff-lined chalkboard, although they are available commercially.

Disadvantages to using the chalkboard are: (1) drawing takes time, (2) you must turn your back to the class, (3) light often glares on the board, (4) it can't be seen by people at the sides of the room, (5) chalk dust ruins records and fouls tape recorders. The overhead projector contains only disadvantage number four. You can write on it while facing the class, and prepared overlays take no class time. This machine is replacing the chalkboard in many classes.

CHARTS

The chart suffers none of the disadvantages of the chalkboard. It can be shown to both sides of the orchestra. When you want a

drawing or a diagram without taking up class time, prepare a
chart.

You can make charts even if your artistic skill is limited. Trace
a picture projected on illustration board. This is one of the best
uses for the opaque projector. This machine has limited use in
class because the room must be very dark.

Mock-ups

A mock-up is a model that is exaggerated to make one particular thing clear. A dummy piano keyboard is a mock-up that em-
phasizes the tactile aspect. A practice pad for drummers is a
mock-up.

Some players make mock-ups of their instrument using spring-
type clothespins. The resistance of the spring forces the fingers to
work hard, thereby developing stronger muscles. An aid of this
type is helpful for cellists and bassists.

A mock-up of a violin can be made from an unservicable instrument. A shallow hole can be drilled in the fingerboard at the
location of every note. This will make the keyboard concept discussed in Chapter 8 clear to the tactile sense of the player in addition to the visual. He can feel how far the finger has to move to
change the pitch a half step, and how far apart two fingers must
be for any interval. He can get the sensation of the notes moving
closer together as his hand moves up the fingerboard. (See Figure
13–1.)

Recordings

The sound of an orchestra playing is meaningful to the student
who plays in one. Whether a recording is a disc made by professionals or a tape made by their own school orchestra, your students can benefit from a lesson using it.

Records can illustrate musical principles you are trying to teach
or a finished performance of a composition being studied. The
sound of any section of the orchestra can be shown in a musical
context. The gamut of music has been recorded, and selections
from it can be obtained easily.

A few pedagogical records have been made. They are valuable
for demonstrating one point at a time, slowly and clearly. They
show the student how his instrument should sound with no dis-

Figure 13–1: VIOLIN MOCK-UP

This violin was fitted with a maple fingerboard stained black. The location of each hole was marked from a fingering chart for violin. A drill press was used for the drilling.

tracting accompaniment. More of these records will be made available if teachers create a demand for them.[1]

The tape recorder as a teaching aid has different characteristics from the record player. The chief advantage is that it can let the students hear themselves as others hear them. Used in conjunction with a record player, it can demonstrate almost anything you might want to show about musical performance.

Following are some things you might tape for your students:

1. A number in rehearsal; players can hear their contribution to the orchestral sound just as you hear it.
2. A professional example of orchestral playing; any one of the PRITT skills can be shown in a carefully chosen excerpt.
3. A professional example of a number they are to study; the use of a recording to introduce a composition was described in Chapter 5.
4. Their orchestra part, played by another student or by you, perhaps at a slow tempo; they could play along.
5. A lecture by, or an interview of, a famous musician; some of these are on radio as intermission features.
6. A selection for study; they can listen with score in hand.
7. Their own individual playing; it is also possible to record them along with a pre-recorded accompaniment if your stereo system has a monitoring feature and headphones.
8. Duplicate tapes of concerts; this requires an additional tape recorder.
9. A lesson; your own canned lesson can be as valuable as a pedagogical record.
10. Your own test of musical aptitude; this can test the musical perception of students in the way you want it tested.

You also will want to tape some things for yourself: a problematic spot that you want to listen to several times; a whole rehearsal to study your rehearsal technique; a rehearsal of concert numbers that you can study to see what improvements are needed; your concerts, for reference in your tape library.

---

[1]Crest Records, Huntingdon Station, N.Y. 11746 produces recorded lessons by famous teachers and performers.

You can purchase a console system to include the equipment necessary to play and record the material you want to use. If cabinetry is not necessary, you can get better components for less money. Figure 13–2 shows a complete system capable of making and playing back tapes from records, radio, or live performance. Radio or record playing in the normal manner is also possible. Figure 13–3 shows an economy system capable of making tapes from records or live performances. It is not possible to play a record with this system; it has to be taped first.

The tape recorder will help you more the better you know how to work it. Study the instruction manual and ask an experienced person to explain taping procedure to you. Practice taping large and small groups. Experiment with microphone placement and volume level setting. Electronic aids need practice for best results much the same as a musical instrument.

The disadvantage to a record for teaching is that it is a finished product. Except for the few available recordings of rehearsals, a record demonstrates the full orchestra playing. The performance is never taken apart or slowed down so we can hear it more clearly.

The main disadvantage to a tape recording is the time it takes to play it back. Rewinding takes only seconds, but that is just enough time to lose the attention of the class.

Playing back everything to the students is poor use of the tape recorder. Only the parts that can teach them something should be played. You can cut the tape and splice these parts together for use in a future lesson. Most of the student's time with you should be spent playing, not listening.

VIDEOTAPE

Videotape equipment is already available to the public so that some people are using it to study their golf swing. All schools should soon see fit to buy it so that teachers can study their teaching.

If your school has been foresighted enough to obtain videotape equipment, use it to study your conducting and rehearsal technique as described in Chapter 12. Do this occasionally to make sure you are developing no bad habits.

Use videotape with string players to show them their bowing

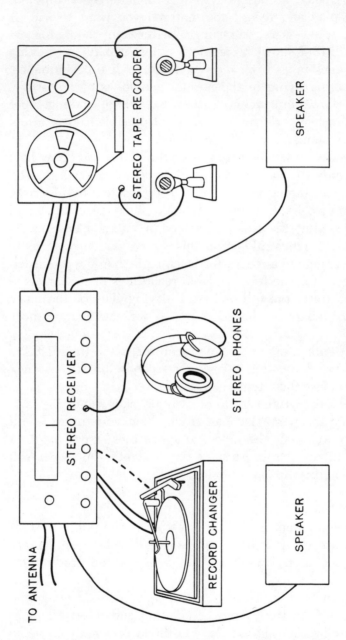

TO ANTENNA

STEREO RECEIVER

STEREO TAPE RECORDER

STEREO PHONES

RECORD CHANGER

SPEAKER

SPEAKER

Figure 13–2: COMPLETE STEREO SYSTEM

The dotted line indicates a ground wire. Power cords are not shown. All wires shown are plugged in; the tape recorder can easily be used separately. This system could be obtained at less cost by deleting AM, using a tape deck instead of a tape recorder, and/or selecting inex-

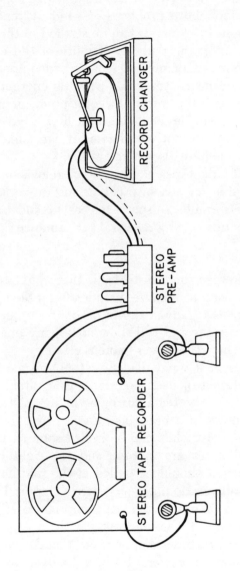

Figure 13–3: ECONOMY STEREO RECORDING SYSTEM
Adding external speakers will make this system quite satisfactory, though it is functional as shown.

and fingering problems from the angle at which these things can best be observed. You have often wished the student could see a process from the angle you see it, and now this is possible through videotape. Embouchure problems of wind players and problems of position on all instruments can be studied in the same manner.

Depending upon the daily availability of the equipment, you might want to make a canned lesson on videotape. As on a pedagogical film, the instructor will always be energetic and patient. He will never rush the lesson, forget a point, or get off the subject. The lesson will be available even if you have a broken arm and laryngitis. A student who missed it can make up this lesson while you are teaching elsewhere.

Commercial videotapes of educational television programs may soon be available for school use. The instant replay feature that we appreciate so much in sports telecasts could be used to great advantage in studying an orchestral performance.

TUNERS

A chromatic electronic instrument that might be used to tune pianos can be used to analyze a student's problems in intonation. The procedure is to adjust the pitch of the tuner to that of the student. The vernier dial will show how many one-hundredths of a semitone (cents) the player's note is errant.

The analysis of a wind player's intonation can be charted to show the deviation of each note from true pitch. This chart can be used to plan a better adjustment of the instrument. For instance, if all notes of a brass instrument using the first valve are sharp, the first valve slide can be pulled somewhat. If a clarinetist's left hand notes are in tune and the right hand notes are sharp, the clarinet should be pulled at the middle joint. You can expect the problematic notes shown in Chapter 11 to be further from true pitch than any other. A compromise in the tuning adjustment will have to be made to get them close enough to be lipped in tune. The tuner can be used to make the student aware of the problematic notes and let him discover how it feels to lip them in tune. The chart of a wind player's pitches will be a profile of intonation deficiencies that will tell him which notes to humor in order to play in tune.[2]

---

[2]*The Intonator*, a pedagogical record with a guide, provides training and practice in matching pitches. Available from Targ & Dinner, Inc., Chicago, Ill.

The tuner can help string players in interval training. First they play a note in tune with the tuner. Then they change to another note and the tuner checks the accuracy of it. This procedure could be used with problematic orchestral passages.

The chromatic tuner that sounds notes is valuable in full orchestra rehearsal (See Figure 13–4.) The pitch of each string can be sounded to help students tune accurately, and it is an instant reference for any note that causes trouble during the rehearsal. The players simply match pitches with the tuner.

Figure 13–4: THE CHROMATIC TUNER
The Peterson Model 300 chromatic tuner sounds all notes in seven octaves, with a vernier dial that adjusts each pitch fifty cents sharp or flat. Photo by the author.

You will undoubtedly think of many ways to use a tuner to better the intonation of your players. Once you use one, you won't want to be without it. One disadvantage is that the acoustically correct frequency sounds flat to our ear in the high range and sharp in the low. Use the vernier dial to compensate for this phenomenon.

RHYTHM TRAINERS

Electronic aids are manufactured for rhythmic reference. They are, in general, several metronomes combined. (See Figure 13–5.) Any division of the beat and/or measure can be illustrated by the clicks. The tone of the clicks is different so that rhythms can be combined.

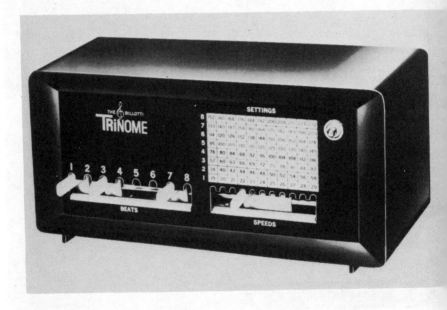

Figure 13–5:   THE BILLOTTI TRINOME
The Billotti Trinome uses three dissimilar beats to reproduce all the varied rhythmic patterns in music at any desired speed. Photo courtesy of Targ & Dinner, Inc., Chicago, Illinois.

The student can be thoroughly involved with such a machine, endeavoring to match its rhythms. A typical teaching procedure is to have the student tap his foot with the pulse set by the trainer. He listens to the rhythm to be played as the trainer indicates it. Then he performs the rhythm in unison with the trainer while tapping his foot.

One traditional problem in teaching rhythm has been in getting the foot to tap the pulse instead of the rhythm being played. Having both rhythm and pulse demonstrated in the rhythm trainer may help the student to solve this problem.

The rhythm trainer can be slowed to the student's learning pace. Then he can practice with it, moving faster one notch at a time until he has the rhythm mastered at the proper tempo.

MOTION PICTURES

Movies are widely used because of the many things they can show. A movie can be a demonstration by an expert player, a concert by an excellent orchestra, or a lesson by a master teacher.[3]

The production of the movie can make things clearer than they would be in a live situation. The slow motion camera can make a swift action detectable in a way that even a skilled demonstrator could not. The size of the image on the screen makes clearer many facets of instrumental technique, especially string and percussion. The technique of animation can show processes that are not visible ordinarily.

A movie of a violin recital is more educational than being there. The action of the bow and fingers can be observed at close range. Finger technique can be seen from the player's point of view and from all other angles.

Movies have the advantage of still pictures too, if your projector has a lever to stop the action. Refocusing is necessary, and the picture is darkened by the heat-absorbing glass that slides behind the film to keep it from burning, but it is worth suffering these inconveniences to be able to stop a film and point out significant details of one scene.

---

[3]One excellent example is *The Violin*, a filmed lesson by Samuel Applebaum, available from University Extension, The University of Wisconsin, Madison, Wisconsin.

Movies have disadvantages, also. They are finished products that can't be changed. Students can't question a movie or move around to get a better view of the subject. The movie shows a complete process that may be beyond the grasp of the students, even in a second showing. A severe disadvantage is the poor sound quality in movie projectors for school use. You can improve this by using an external speaker better than the one supplied with the projector.

Isolated scenes can better be shown with still pictures. These are convenient in filmstrip form, and some of these have a recorded sound track. Scores of some compositions are available on filmstrips.

The orchestra as a teaching aid

Your orchestra is an audio-visual aid for teaching the young audiences of your school district. When you present a program to them, you are really giving a lesson about orchestral music. Young people can be guided to understand better what they are hearing if you use the orchestra effectively as the complete audio-visual aid it can be.

Leonard Bernstein's *Young People's Concerts* have set an example for us to follow. The general format for his programs—explaining, taking the music apart, and finally playing a whole piece through—conforms to the preparation—presentation—follow-up steps advocated for all teaching aids. The young students learn the significance of a musical item, they hear it clearly demonstrated, and then they hear it in context.

During a presentation to an elementary school audience, you won't want to spend a lot of time introducing and talking about each number. This won't be necessary if you let the school music teacher prepare the students for what you will present. You might prepare a list or a tape recording of things you would like the young people to know before the concert. As a follow-up activity, you could leave a tape of the uninterrupted concert for use by the classroom teachers.

14 PUBLIC PERFORMANCES

The presentation of a program to an audience is the climax of many hours of preparation. As far as the director is concerned, the educational goals have been met before the concert, but the performance is the goal toward which the students have worked. This immediate goal makes orchestra one of the few subjects where the student is learning material for the present instead of the future. Performances for the public build morale and provide an incentive for the students to learn the music and play their instrument well. Every step should be taken to insure a successful concert.

Performances for school audiences increase the musical understanding of all the students. This is one of the main justifications for the school orchestra program, and it should not be neglected.

Taking the players to perform in an auditorium away from their school requires special equipment and organization. The instruments and accessories must be made portable, and arrangements have to be made for the physical set-up of the orchestra in the unfamiliar auditorium. The details of such a tour can best be handled by the orchestra conductor. Remembering to do everything is difficult. The check lists in this chapter should be helpful.

Scheduling performances

The performances for the year should be scheduled in advance to avoid conflicts. September is a good time. Steer clear of other school activities; the players won't be able to perform their best

the day after the junior prom. Make up your schedule using a calendar marked with all school holidays, major school activities,
teachers' conventions, festivals scheduled by your Music Educators' Association, and holidays for all religions. Remember that
Jewish holidays begin at sundown on the day previous to the one
marked on the calendar. Avoid having concerts that conflict with
other local musical organizations. Also try not to schedule concerts on evenings that some of your students will be rehearsing
with the local symphony orchestra. Make your dates public as
soon as possible so that no one later schedules activities that
conflict with your concerts.

You may be in doubt about how many public performances to
present during the school year. The number depends upon so
many variables that you will not be certain. Schedule the maximum number you think will be possible, since it is easier to cancel
some than it is to find open dates later in the year.

Owing to the time involved in getting organized at the beginning of the year, you probably will not be able to perform a full
concert before December. (See Figure 14–1.) A concert before
the Easter recess and one before the end of school can be prepared if you have daily rehearsals. Schedule the last concert near
the end of school so you won't have many rehearsals left after the
final program; the students regard these rehearsals as unimportant. Leave some rehearsals to work on music for graduation exercises. Choosing easy music with a small orchestration will enable
you to have the orchestra play without the senior class members.
Besides these performances, you may want to schedule a concert
of solos and ensembles to give many students a chance to show
their accomplishments in small groups.

You might present more concerts if your orchestra doesn't have
to prepare the full program. A joint concert with the vocal music
department helps to relieve much of the pressure from both
groups. You can select the numbers the orchestra performs best,
and the players will have ample endurance for the short program.
Also, a larger audience is attracted because of the number of performers, and there is the musical possibility of combining the
groups for a selection.

A festival performance featuring many of the musical groups
of the school district spreads the work among several groups. A

Figure 14-1: THE EWING HIGH SCHOOL ORCHESTRA
The smiles tell the story of this first public performance of the year by the Ewing High School Orchestra, Lloyd Snyder, director.

performance of this magnitude must be scheduled far in advance. It involves planning of musical matters in addition to the logistics of moving the groups on and off the performing area. The music to be used should be agreed upon when the performance is scheduled so the younger musicians will have time to learn it.

Scheduling concerts for school audiences in between public performances keeps up the morale of the orchestra. The shorter program you will use can consist of numbers from your review list as outlined in Chapter 5.

The concert program

A school orchestra program is different from that of a symphony orchestra. The musical appreciation that most school orchestra players and their audience have is not on a level to enable them to enjoy an all-symphonic concert. If you teach in a very enlightened community, you may want to present all numbers of symphonic caliber, but normal situations call for different programming. The rounded musical education that you are trying to provide for the students demands an exposure to all types of orchestral music.

Nothing is further from the spirit of school music than an all-Beethoven, all-modern, or all-anything program. Even if you plan enough Beethoven during the year for a full concert of his works, it would be better to put one number on each program.

An intermission in a concert lets the orchestra rest and the audience relax. A club from the school would be glad to sell refreshments. The intermission also provides time for any stage changes that have to be made.

School orchestra concerts should be shorter than professional performances. A short, varied program will be representative of your work with the students and enjoyable for the audience. The players will get through the performance without straining, and your rehearsals can be more thorough if there are not so many numbers to be prepared.

Concert programming starts when you put the music into the orchestra folios. Including representative compositions from several periods of music history and from various categories as listed in Chapter 3 would give you a wide range of possible program numbers. Preliminary selection of those to be included is a matter of elimination. Eliminate: (1) numbers that can't be ready on time, (2) arrangements that don't sound good with your orchestra, (3) overlong or repetitious selections, (4) one of two numbers that closely resemble each other.

The next step is to select a program of proper length that shows the range of music you have explored with the students. A typical one would include an overture, a selection or two from the standard repertoire, a modern composition, a solo, and lighter works: a light classic, a Latin-American dance, perhaps a march, a novelty, and selections from a Broadway show. A patriotic selection could be a grand finale.

Once the concert numbers are selected, the arrangement of them on the program becomes important. The order of the typical program just listed is good because it presents the challenging numbers while the orchestra and audience are still fresh. It has variety because of the different nature of all the selections. The plan of it is to use the full orchestra for an impressive beginning, offer the difficult works, the solo, and then the lighter works. The same plan could be used even if you prefer not to include lighter works; substitute short classics or an exciting long piece with a grandiose ending.

No matter what the numbers are, the program will be more effective if they are arranged to take advantage of the variety that exists between them. Tonality, tempo, meter, style, mood, and orchestration are items to consider when deciding which numbers should follow each other. It is possible that half of the numbers you select might be in the key of D. Numbers should be inserted between them to keep the key of D from becoming commonplace. A waltz and a minuet might provide historical contrast, but monotony will set in if they are paired on the concert.

Styles of composition are sure to vary, especially if you have several periods of musical history represented. The danger here is in being anticlimactic. Mozart will sound pale after Rossini, Khachaturian and Copland.

A subtle point that bears on program order is the effect that the key at the end of one number has on the beginning of the next. A lively number will sound more so if it is in the key having a dominant relationship to the one just ended. A pastoral composition will be more peaceful if it is in the subdominant relation to the end of the previous selection. If you are unsure of the effect the end of one number will have on the beginning of another, tape the end of it several times, following it each time by the beginning of a different number. Study the recordings to decide which number should follow.

Stage fright

The excitement of playing for an audience can make players nervous. Overcoming this stage fright is difficult. Discussing it doesn't help; in fact, it makes the students more self-conscious.

An unexcited conductor is a steadying influence. It is important that everything is organized and under control so that the conductor can be calm and relaxed. All the arrangements of stage set-up, stage crew, light crew, microphones, announcer, programs, ushers, ticket personnel, recording equipment and personnel, photographer, and other special equipment or personnel you may use should be made in advance so there are no last-minute details to arrange.

You as a conductor will be calm if you accept realistically what will happen in the concert. The performance will be better than the average rehearsal, yet not as good as the best one. The mistakes made will be some of the same ones that were made in rehearsals, but mostly ones that were never made before. Hoping for an errorless performance can set you on edge. Worrying about each mistake as it is made in a concert can cause you to make conducting mistakes or even to lose your place.

Concert night should find you relaxed and content. Your teaching work is done, and all you have to do is run through it once for the audience. There's nothing you can do on concert night to improve the results significantly. Your only thought should be to make your performance as a conductor as accurate and as musical as you can.

The stage fright problem is greater with small groups and greatest with soloists. There is only one preventive: they must be able to play their selection with no trouble at all. If they have trouble getting through it in rehearsal, they are likely to break down completely in performance. Extra rehearsal after the piece is learned reassures the players. If they broke down five times in a certain spot, that spot should be played ten times to make sure it won't happen again. Thorough knowledge of the composition being played will enable them to recover if they do break down. Train them to enter at a new phrase and most of the audience will never know something was left out.

Soloists

The solo with orchestral accompaniment provides an outlet for the expression of a talented student. It also serves to teach the orchestra members some points of musical finesse—a pointed lesson when it comes from one of their classmates. Solos are excellent program material because they captivate the interest of an audience. Also, the accompaniment to a solo usually can be worked out quicker than a concert piece because the orchestra is not burdened with the melody most of the time.

The selection of a solo for a student is often a point of disagreement. Listening to a professional recording, the student thinks, "That doesn't sound so hard," and he wants to play a major concerto. You must talk him into playing a movement of an easy concerto or, better yet, a student concerto. His private teacher may suggest something, but you and the student must agree upon the choice. Many times the matter will hinge upon whether the orchestra can learn the accompaniment. This is particularly true of rented accompaniments that have a time limit.

Youth concerts

The orchestra members appreciate the chance to make use of their learning by playing concert numbers for a different audience. The young people of the school district enjoy seeing an orchestra perform, especially one that they might join some day. Older students enjoy seeing what their friends in the orchestra are able to do, and it is a part of their general education to hear a concert occasionally. Have some lighter numbers for the end of these concerts.

You might give a concert for a school audience outside your school district. This might be part of an exchange whereby the orchestra or band from the other school presents a concert for your student body. Arrange an exchange concert through the music teacher if you know him; otherwise have your principal arrange it.

There are many things you can do in a concert for a school audience. For little children you can demonstrate the instruments, show how they sound in different combinations, and play short selections from your concert program. For older children you can explain the selections and play them, as suggested in Chapter 13.

Students in all grades need to have their listening directed to keep them interested in the concert. They need detailed descriptions of the features of the music being played. It helps if the main themes are demonstrated before the performance. You can also include information about the composer. His early years should be of interest to young people. Let them know what he was able to do when he was their age.

The orchestra tour

A tour can be as short as a single concert in a school one mile away or as long as a series of concerts throughout the state. Anytime the orchestra presents a concert outside its home school, preparations must be made to make sure everything goes well.

There are many things to arrange: the date, time, and place for the performance(s); permission for the students to go; transportation; transportation of baggage, instruments, music, and accessories; meals and housing. You must arrange these things, double-check the arrangements, and supervise the carrying-out of each detail. On a tour of more than one day, several student and adult assistants will be needed.

Answers to the following questions will be a basis for making the necessary arrangements.

1. What are the directions for getting to the concert location? Where should we enter the building?
2. How much travel time is necessary, allowing extra time in case of delay?
3. At what time is our arrival expected?
4. What time is each performance scheduled?
5. How long will each performance be?
6. When and where will the players eat and sleep? What will the financial arrangements be?
7. When will we start back to our school?

Using the answers to the above questions you can plan:

1. Time of departure (Allow time for loading.)
2. Instructions to players about meals and housing
3. Instructions to drivers
4. Time schedule for concerts (Allow time for warm-up and tuning.)
5. Arrival time back at school (Arrange for the building to be open for unloading.)

Students should be made responsible for their instrument, accessories, and music. Players of large instruments should check to see that their instrument has been loaded and that no accessories have been left behind. The first-chair percussionist should use a check list for this. You should also make a check list for items that you have to remember. Include your baton, your music, the electronic tuner, the repair kit, and extra strings. Trust that local repairmen will be available to handle anything out of the ordinary.

To avoid the embarrassment of arriving unexpectedly, make sure you have a letter confirming the date and time of all concerts. If arrangements have been made verbally, send a letter ahead to confirm the day, hour, and date of the performance. List the time you will arrive, the equipment you will expect to find ready, the time you will be ready to perform, and the duration of the concert.

If possible, inspect the auditoriums in which you will play. Take note of any special problems you will encounter. Make sure enough music stands and chairs will be available at all concert locations. If you want to use some of the large instruments of a school you will visit, confirm their availability by letter or phone.

It is very important to instruct the students thoroughly about their responsibilities on the tour. They must know exactly what to take along for the musical task they have to do. Also helpful is a list of personal items that will be necessary. You will have to remind them of the conduct you expect. One important item is that they should stay with the group until you have dismissed them. Make sure that they know when and where to be ready for the next performance before you dismiss them.

A fast set-up plan helps on a tour, especially when you arrive later than expected. Each student should know what he's expected to do to help. You can practice this by dismissing the orchestra from the rehearsal room to set up in the auditorium of your school.

An easier tour to arrange is performances in elementary classrooms by a small ensemble. This intimate setting lets the students ask questions about the instruments, and they get to see and hear them up close. Perhaps some class members could try a few notes on an instrument. Take extra students to carry music stands and chairs. Arrange an alternate date in case of the absence of a player.

The pit orchestra

Some rewarding experiences in playing in an orchestra come when the music is a part of a bigger production, one that involves action onstage. Having the orchestra participate brings it closer to the other subjects and co-curricular activities.

The Broadway musical is currently a popular endeavor in many high schools. The orchestra parts that are rented are the original ones played on Broadway. A well-trained orchestra can manage them by omitting difficult passages.

A variety show lacks the continuity of the musical play, and this makes it somewhat easier to produce. It might include ballet, vocal and instrumental solos, tumbling acts and comedy acts. The orchestra can play separate selections in addition to accompanying the various acts.

Incidental music at a dramatic play can add to the production. Choose music in keeping with the play. Even though the music is not played during the action, it should set the mood.

Festival performances

Arranging a local festival requires the hard work and cooperation of all the music teachers, administrators, and custodial staff. Provisions for seating the large number of performers and onlookers must be made. Amplification of the performing groups may be necessary. A rehearsal will have to be arranged so that all participants know where to be at all times.

To make a festival beneficial to the students, each group should hear every other group perform. They can combine in a grand finale if parts are adapted for the younger players. The planning of the music will require meetings of the music teachers.

Annual orchestra festivals are arranged by your state organization of music teachers affiliated with the Music Educators National Conference. A few students from each school in the state come together to form an orchestra. This orchestra rehearses several days and presents a concert. The experience is a memorable one for the students involved. Each county also may hold a festival, and sometimes several counties go together to sponsor a district festival so that more students get a chance to participate.

Another type of orchestra festival brings together full orchestras. They serve as an audience for each other. Fraternization between the players and the comments of the judges supplement the experience of hearing other orchestras perform. It builds the morale of your players to know that so many people are interested in orchestra.

Publicity

Many people who don't even attend your concert will still be affected by the publicity that you give it. People of the community should know that their school has an orchestra capable of presenting a concert. Some of these may even start their young children on instruments so that they can one day play in your orchestra.

If a newsletter listing the dates of school activities is sent home to parents, make sure your concert dates are on it. You may want to put out a special flyer to publicize the concert. Flyers can be passed out in shopping centers, placed behind doorknobs of homes and cars, and/or distributed to homerooms for each student to take home.

Publicity within the school can be accomplished easily. Announcements in the daily bulletin and over the central sound system are effective. If an issue of the school newspaper will be out prior to a concert, orchestra members who are on the newspaper staff will see that the concert receives publicity there.

If the art department or art club would make posters publicizing the concert, the orchestra members would find most merchants willing to display them. Making these for every concert becomes a burden, however, and if you want posters, investigate the possibility of having them made commercially.

A billboard on the school property advertises events effectively.

Every time parents pass the school, they will be reminded of the coming event. Removable letters such as those used on theater marquees make the changing of the message easy. Advertise early; the repeated seeing of the announcement puts it across. Remove the message promptly when the concert is over.

Local radio and television stations usually provide a time for free announcements in the public interest. People who are interested in their community listen to these broadcasts. Newspapers will print announcements of unusual school activities—sometimes a full article complete with pictures. You can contact these news media easily with a form letter. Blank spaces make it usable year after year. Figure 14–2 is a sample.

```
                        News Release


    On _____, _____, 19___, the Ewing High

School Orchestra of Ewing Township, Trenton, New Jersey,

will present a concert in the school auditorium at

Parkway and Olden Avenues.  The concert will feature a

composition entitled _____ in addition

to selections of all types.  Featured as _____

soloist will be _____ _____, a student in the

_____ class.  You are cordially invited to attend.

Admission will be _____.  The concert starts at ____ P.M.
```

Figure 14–2

Most people who attend the concert will do so because they know a performer. Exhort the orchestra members to "talk-up the concert" to friends, neighbors, and relatives. Playing a concert is something special that people will find interesting. The chief advantage in selling tickets door-to-door is the effective publicity. The personal contact of orchestra members within the community makes the inhabitants cognizant of the value the orchestra has for the students.

A check list of publicity media will insure your considering each one as a means of advertising the upcoming concert. Figure 14–3 is a sample. Your standard news release form could be filled out and mailed to many of the places on the check list.

A publicity committee from the orchestra could do much of the work involved. These people could handle the news release forms, perhaps rewriting them to suit the medium to be used.

The printed program

The program for your concert can be anything from a mimeographed sheet to a multi-page printed booklet. It can include ads (they help defray printing costs), program notes, and announcements of future musical events in the school district. Credits should be given by listing the names of all people who helped in preparing the concert: orchestra members, stage crew, lighting crew, ushers, recording technicians, announcers, printer, cover designer, and any other people directly connected with the presentation. Be sure to include the date on the program for your future reference.

The program page itself should list each composition and its subdivisions, the composer, and the arranger, if any. Soloists should be listed under the composition they perform.

Program notes are traditionally separate from the program page. People who arrive early like to read them, and these paragraphs give you a chance to impart information that will help the audience to understand the music better. You can also have an announcer read program notes between numbers. This eliminates the need for people to try to read in a darkened auditorium. Another benefit is the rest the players get while the announcer reads.

Students should help with the program as much as possible. Artistic students can design the cover, those interested in dramatics can take turns announcing, and those with literary aspirations can write the program notes and prepare the program for printing.

Students can be taught to write good program notes by answering the following questions:

1. Why is the piece titled as it is?

Publicity Checklist

Concert date on school calendar _____

Flyers distributed:

    to homerooms _____

    door to door _____

    cars _____

    shopping center _____

School public address system announcements _____

Notices in the daily bulletin:

    high school _____

    junior high # 1 _____ # 2 _____

    elementary # 1 _____ # 2 _____ # 3 _____

School newspaper

Posters _____

Radio stations:

    WWO _____

    WOK _____

    WWAJ _____

Television stations:

    Channel 5 _____

    Channel 13 _____

Newspapers:

    Daily Times _____

    Morning Tribune _____

Tickets distributed _____

"Talk-it-up" speech to orchestra _____

2. Is there a story to it?
3. What outstanding musical features does it have?
4. Was there a special reason for the composer's writing it?
5. For what was the composer most famous?
6. What did the arranger do to the composition?

These are the normal questions adults have about a composition. Any more details than these begins to sound like a lecture.

You will want the program along with a tape recording of the concert in your files. Also include a photograph of the group as another reminder of the people you worked with for so many hours.

BIBLIOGRAPHY

Apel, Willi, *Harvard Dictionary of Music*. Cambridge, Mass.: Harvard University Press, 1944, Thirteenth Printing, 1961.

Bartholomew, Wilmer T., *Acoustics of Music*. New York, N.Y.: Prentice-Hall, Inc., 1942.

Dale, Edgar, *Audio-Visual Methods in Teaching*. New York, N.Y.: Holt, Rinehart, and Winston, Revised Edition, 1954.

Fussell, Raymond C., *Exercises for Ensemble Drill*. Minneapolis, Minn.: Schmitt, Hall & McCreary Company, 1938.

Galamian, Ivan, *Principles of Violin Playing and Teaching*. Englewood Cliffs, N.J., Prentice-Hall, Inc., 1962.

Gary, Charles L., ed., *Music Buildings, Rooms, and Equipment*. Washington, D.C.: Music Educators National Conference, 1966.

Green, Elizabeth A. H., *The Modern Conductor*. Englewood Cliffs, N.J.: Prentice-Hall, Inc., 1961.

Green, Elizabeth A. H., *Teaching Stringed Instruments in Classes*. Englewood Cliffs, N.J.: Prentice-Hall, Inc., 1966.

House, Robert W., *Instrumental Music for Today's Schools*. Englewood Cliffs, N.J.: Prentice-Hall, Inc., 1965.

Hutton, Truman, *Improving the School String Section*. New York, N.Y.: Carl Fischer, Inc., 1963.

Magnell, Elmer P., *68 Pares Studies*. Rockville Centre, N.Y.: Belwin, Inc., 1957.

Pottle, Ralph R., *Tuning the School Band and Orchestra*. Hammond, La.: Privately published, Second Edition, 1962.

Razey, Don H., *How to File and Find Music*. Philadelphia, Pa.: J. W. Pepper & Son, Inc., 1966.

Rothrock, Carson, "Scheduling Lessons in Ensembles," *Music Educators Journal*, Vol. 53, No. 9 (May, 1967), 60.

Rudolf, Max, *The Grammar of Conducting*. New York, N.Y.: G. Schirmer, Inc., 1950.

Yaus, Grover C., *101 Rhythmic Rest Patterns*. Rockville Centre, N.Y.: Belwin, Inc., 1953.

Books for the music department library

Accompaniments Unlimited 1970 Catalog. Grosse Pointe Woods, Mich.: Accompaniments Unlimited, Inc., 1969.

Apel, Willi, and Archibald T. Davison, *Historical Anthology of Music*. Cambridge, Mass.: Harvard University Press, Revised Edition, 1949, Eighth Printing, 1966.

Applebaum, Samuel and Sada, *With the Artists*. New York, N.Y.: John Markert & Co., 1955.

Baker, Theodore, *Baker's Biographical Dictionary of Musicians*. 5th Edition Revised by N. Slonimsky, New York, N.Y.: G. Schirmer, Inc., 1958.

Bessom, Malcolm, *Supervising the Successful School Music Program*. West Nyack, N.Y.: Parker Publishing Company, Inc. 1969.

Brand, Erick D., *Band Instrument Repairing Manual*. Elkhart, Indiana: Privately published, fourth edition, 1946.

Camden, Archie, *Bassoon Technique*. London: Oxford University Press, 1962.

Cassell's Italian Dictionary. New York, N.Y.: Funk & Wagnalls Company, Inc., 1958.

Cassell's New German Dictionary. New York, N.Y.: Funk & Wagnalls Company, Inc., 1965.

Chapman, F. B., *Flute Technique*. London: Oxford University Press, third edition, 1958.

Collins, Myron D. and John E. Green, *Playing and Teaching Percussion Instruments*. Englewood Cliffs, N.J.: Prentice-Hall, Inc. 1962.

Curtis, Robert E., *Your Future in Music*. New York, N.Y.: Richards Rosen Press, Inc., 1962.

Ewen, David, *Complete Book of 20th Century Music*. Englewood Cliffs, N.J.: Prentice-Hall, Inc., second edition, 1959.

Farkas, Philip, *The Art of Brass Playing*. Bloomington, Ind.: Brass Publications, 1962.

Franz, Frederick, *Metronome Techniques*. New Haven, Conn.: Privately published, 1947.

Geiger, Leroy, *How to Make Your Own Violin*. Cleveland, Ohio. Ernst Heinrich Roth Co., Inc., 1963.

Grout, Donald J., *History of Western Music*. New York, N.Y.: W. W. Norton & Co., 1960.

Lacy, Gene, *Organizing and Developing the High School Orchestra*. West Nyack, N.Y.: Parker Publishing Co., 1971.

Leeder, Joseph A., and William S. Haynie, *Music Education in the High School*. Englewood Cliffs, N.J.: Prentice-Hall, Inc., 1958.

Lehman, Paul R., *Tests and Measurements in Music*. Englewood Cliffs, N.J.: Prentice-Hall, Inc., 1968.

Mansion's Shorter French and English Dictionary. New York, N.Y.: Henry Holt and Co., n.d.

Marrero, Isabelo Ernesto, *Drumming the Latin-American Way*. New York, N.Y.: Edward B. Marks Music Corp., 1949.

McMillen, Hugh E., *A Guide to Bass Trombone Playing*. Fullerton, Cal.: F. E. Olds & Son, 1953.

Moses, Harry, *Developing and Administering a Comprehensive High School Music Program*. West Nyack, N.Y.: Parker Publishing Co., 1970.

Orchestra Music Guide. Evanston, Ill.: The Instrumentalist Co., 1966.

Paulson, Joseph, *Get in Rhythm*. Westbury, N.Y.: Pro Art Publications, Inc., 1948.

Pence, Homer, *Teacher's Guide to the Bassoon*. Elkhart, Ind.: H. & A. Selmer, Inc., 1963.

Rimsky-Korsakov, Nikolay, *Principles of Orchestration*. New York, N.Y.: Dover Publications, Inc., 1964.

Rothwell, Evelyn, *Oboe Technique*. London: Oxford University Press, 1953, reprinted 1964.

Schonberg, Harold C., *The Great Conductors*. New York, N.Y.: Simon and Schuster, 1967.

Schuller, Gunther, *Horn Technique*. London: Oxford University Press, 1962.

Schwann Long Playing Record Catalog. Boston, Mass.: W. Schwann, Inc., 1971.

Scuorzo, Herbert, *Practical Audio-Visual Handbook for Teachers*. West Nyack, N.Y.: Parker Publishing Company, Inc., 1967.

Thurston, Frederick, *Clarinet Technique*. London: Oxford University Press, 1964.

Organizations of interest to school orchestra directors

American Guild of Double Bass Players
c/o Mr. Lucas Drew, School of Music, University of Miami,
Coral Gables, Florida 33124

American String Teachers Association
c/o Mr. Robert Marince, Lawrence Twp. Public Schools,
2455 Princeton Pike, Trenton, N.J. 08638

Music Educators National Conference
1201 Sixteenth St. N.W., Washington, D.C. 20036

National School Orchestra Association
c/o Orville Dally, 633 Center St., Bryan, Ohio 43506

INDEX